Introduction to Sensors in IoT and Cloud Computing Applications

Authored by

Ambika Nagaraj

Department of Computer Applications,
SSMRV College,
Bangalore,
India

Introduction to Sensors in IoT and Cloud Computing Applications

Author: Ambika Nagaraj

ISBN (Online): 978-981-14-7935-9

ISBN (Print): 978-981-14-7933-5

ISBN (Paperback): 978-981-14-7934-2

need for a court order if at any point you breach any terms of this License Agreement. In no event will any delay or failure by Bentham Science Publishers in enforcing your compliance with this License Agreement constitute a waiver of any of its rights.

3. You acknowledge that you have read this License Agreement, and agree to be bound by its terms and conditions. To the extent that any other terms and conditions presented on any website of Bentham Science Publishers conflict with, or are inconsistent with, the terms and conditions set out in this License Agreement, you acknowledge that the terms and conditions set out in this License Agreement shall prevail.

Bentham Science Publishers Pte. Ltd.
80 Robinson Road #02-00
Singapore 068898
Singapore
Email: subscriptions@benthamscience.net

CONTENTS

FOREWORD 1

"The Internet of Things is the present and the future. It is composed of Smart Objects, objects, and sensors interconnecting between themselves to make actions and take measures of almost anything, anytime, and anywhere, and to automate different parts of our life. However, we need to manage all the generated data. Data that are from different parts of the world and data that can be accessed from anywhere. This is where Cloud Computing can help us to manage this big problem. Cloud Computing allows anybody to access data from anywhere. Besides, it provides us with different tools and 'infinite' capacity for storage and processing. Then, the Internet of Things and sensors need Cloud Computing, and Cloud Computing can provide us with tools to work with them."

Cristian González García
University of Oviedo
Asturias
Spain

FOREWORD 2

"It is a distinct pleasure to write a foreword to this important new book "Introduction to Sensors in IoT and Cloud Computing Applications", authored by Professor (Dr.) N.Ambika. This book is well designed and assembled an impressive and substantive array of important topics to explore recent advances in Sensors in Internet of Things (IoT) and Cloud Computing Applications.

It is the product of author Professor N.Ambika who is well-suited to tackle its subject-matter as she is an educator with vast experiences in the field of computer science, Sensor Network, IoT and Cloud Computing. This book consists of six chapters with the first Chapter beginning with Introduction and applications of sensors whereas the last chapter summarized the integrated system, its applications and open issues. After introduction, the First Chapter provides an overview of applications of sensors. Second Chapter discusses architecture and working of IoT, use cases, challenges the technology is facing and future directions. Third Chapter presents security issues, management issues, advantages, applications, challenges, and future directions. The fourth Chapter discusses the taxonomy, challenges and future directions and the fifth chapter summarizes the integrated system, its applications and some of the open issues.

Sensors in IoT and Cloud Computing is a fast-emerging area of computer science and communication significantly focused in recent past few years. IoT and Cloud Computing works towards growing efficiency of day to day tasks and both have paired connection, presents a great opportunity and influences several domains of modern technologies wherein IoT and Cloud Computing can be used including Smart home, Smart City, Industrial Internet, Connect Car and Intelligent Transport System *etc*.

I would like to congratulate the author for this wonderful effort, which will be very much beneficial to academics, research scholars, IoT and Cloud Computing analysts, Post graduate, graduate and undergraduate level students of Computer Science and Engineering, Electronics and Communication Engineering, Computer Applications and Information and Communication Technology and recommend this book for university textbook and a comprehensive research handbook."

Dr. Nirbhay Chaubey, SMIEE
Dean of Computer Science
Ganpat University
India

FOREWORD 3

"This book is written by an author who is skilled in the subject. The author has good experience in this field. The book covered the latest technologies such as IoT and Cloud Computing. This book will be helpful to the reader to know about sensors, internet of things and Cloud computing. The organization of this book is good."

Dr. Mansaf Alam
Editor-in-Chief
Journal of Applied Information Science

&

Associate Professor &
Young Faculty Research Fellow
DietY, Govt. of India
Department of Computer Science
Jamia Millia Islamia, New Delhi
India

PREFACE

Ongoing advances in micro-electro-mechanical systems (MEMS) innovation, remote interchanges, and computerized gadgets have empowered the improvement of ease, low-power, multifunctional sensor hubs that are little in the estimate and impart untethered in short separations. These little sensor hubs, which comprise detecting, information preparing, and conveying parts, influence the possibility of sensor systems dependent on community exertion of an enormous number of hubs.

Intelligent sensors are worked as IoT segments that convert this present reality variable that they're estimating into a computerized information stream for transmission to a gateway. Internet of Things (IoT) applications, regardless of whether for city foundations, plants, or wearable gadgets utilize enormous varieties of sensors gathering information for transmission over the Internet to a local, cloud-based figuring asset. Investigation programming running on the cloud PCs lessens the enormous volumes of created information into noteworthy data for clients, and directions to actuators retreat in the field. The integration of the three has provided ease as well as huge profit for various businesses. The book provides an insight into the different technologies – sensors, Internet-of-things (IoT), and cloud computing. The technologies join hand-in-hand to build a better system aiding betterment to society. The integration has aided in building a robust system yielding profitable business to all the stockholders.

This book is a collection of various suggestions provided by the authors towards sensors, IoT, cloud, and integration technology. The chapters summaries the use of the technology in various applications, shortcomings and future directions suggested by various authors. The collection is profitable for young readers providing better insight into various technologies, researchers and students.

I would like to thank Bentham Science publications for providing me an opportunity to write this book. I would like to thank my college management for their support and cooperation. I would also like to thank my family and friends for their encouragement.

CONSENT FOR PUBLICATION

Not applicable.

CONFLICT OF INTEREST

The authors declare no conflict of interest, financial or otherwise.

ACKNOWLEDGEMENTS

Declared none.

Ambika Nagaraj
MCA, M.Phil, Ph.D
Department of Computer Applications
SSMRV College, Bangalore
India

CHAPTER 1

Introduction to Sensors

Abstract: Sensors are tiny, low-cost devices engaging themselves to monitor the environment in many applications. Their assembly is programmed to gather sensory information and move data to the predefined destination. The readings received by the sensors are gathered by the gateway node and redirected to the data processing module. They further parse the directions and send the information to the Sink node. This chapter details the working of these devices in various applications and the challenges faced by them. It also provides an overview of the book. Like any domain or sensors that have shortcomings are worked upon to provide flexibility and ease.

Keywords: Applications, Challenges, Wireless sensor network.

INTRODUCTION

Wireless Sensor Network (WSN) [1] known as Micro-Electro-Mechanical Systems (MEMS) [2] is the collection of smart devices. The nodes in this distribution are spatial to perform an application-oriented task. This development is a result of the miniaturization of computing and sensing technologies that enables the growth of low-power and inexpensive instruments. These tiny devices are deployed in the environment to monitor or track any object of interest. Their deployment in the network is in an inactive state. They self-configure, communicate with the nodes within the short-range, and constitute their topology. Sensors are assembly collection of the conceivably high number of detecting nodes, imparting remote multi-jump design [3]. Exceptional nodes called cluster heads [4] assemble the results and forward them to the next available hop. They aid in infrastructure failures, conserve natural resources, increase productivity, enhance security, and enable the growth of a new series of applications. Depending on the type of network they are deployed in, the sink and the node count vary in number. It collects the required readings, processes them, and disseminates them. They monitor real-time physical conditions, including temperature, humidity, sound, intensity, and vibration. Another positive aspect is that these devices can go global by giving live readings of the environment. Like every technology, these sensors also carry the burden of their drawbacks. Energy, power, security, storage space are some of the disadvantages that need working.

Ambika Nagaraj

BACKGROUND

Wireless Sensor Network (WSN) can understand the short-distance correspondence between their community devices by building remote systems in impromptu habits. It is troublesome to associate them and versatile correspondence systems (Internet). It is because of its absence of uniform institutionalization in correspondence conventions. The detection advancements and the information from WSN cannot be transmitted in long separation considering the constraint of WSN transmission conventions. Internet-of-Things (IoT) provided an answer to these questions. Thus, with the improvement of the Internet-of-Things, another system gear called the Internet-of-Things Gateway is developed. Their objective is to settle with the heterogeneity between different sensor systems and portable correspondence systems. It also fortifies the administration of the WSN with the terminal device and scaffolds customary correspondence systems with sensor systems. The procedure makes it easier to deal with the gadgets of sensor systems.

Internet-of-Things is a dynamic and a Global Networked Infrastructure arrangement that manages self-designing nodes with high Intelligence. Intelligent sensors work together to convert this present reality variable and transmit the estimated values into a digital information stream for transmission to a passage. The inherent microchip unit knowledge usage in different capacities has made it acceptable. It can decrease the heap on its progressively focal assets. They can detect any creation parameters that begin to float past satisfactory standards and produce alerts in like manner. These devices made of large little items are with a constrained Memory stockpiling and computing limit. Their description of an authentic world is noteworthy in regards to Privacy, Performance, Scalability, and Reliability.

Another issue that the sensors face is low memory capacity. Cloud infrastructure provides answers to these issues faced by the sensor technology. Cloud Computing is an immense future with unlimited storage, considering stockpiling and calculation controls. Distributed computing is a plan of action to engage ubiquitously, on-request organization access to an assortment of configurable figuring assets. Some of the examples include stockpiling, administrations, maintaining servers, and applications that can immediately provide noteworthy administration. Cloud computing has been innovative with notable suggestions for the conveyance of the Internet. Information supervision by cloud administrations secures the system. It can supervise an enormous number of gadgets and hence help the maintenance of large scale assembly and its applications.

Distributed computing, on wheels, is known as Mobile cloud computing. With the blast of portable applications and the help of Cloud computing, the system handles an assortment of administrations for versatile clients. Mobile clients amass rich experience of different administrations from versatile applications. These systems run on the gadgets as well as on remote servers through the isolated systems. Lately, practices focused on cell phones have begun getting inexhaustible with applications of different classes. Some examples include amusement, games, business, informal communication, travel, and news.

The fog adds extra fuel to cloud technology. It empowers the computation at the edge of the system. It can convey new executions and administrations. In fog processing, offices or foundations that are assets to administrations on the verge of the system are called fog devices. The switches can work as the latest servers.

WORKING OF SENSORS IN DIFFERENT APPLICATIONS

The ongoing development of the Micro-Electro-Mechanical Systems (MEMS) [1, 5, 6] and remote correspondence innovation makes it to convey on an enormous scale, low power, reasonable sensory organization. Such a methodology guarantees an advantage over the traditional detecting techniques in numerous ways. The large-scale organization has not just expanded spatial inclusion and accomplishes higher goals, but it also builds the adaptation to non-critical failure of the framework. The system makes it much increasingly appealing in military applications [7] and other hazard related applications like territory checking and ecological perception [8]. Fig. (**1**) portrays the implementation of the wireless sensor network. The exercise in the blue box uses different technologies in an assembly. The applications in the green box can use the same category of devices. The practice is widely used and explained below.

Intrusion Detection

An intrusion identification framework recognizes and reports a suspected activity in its discovery region. These frameworks are regularly coordinated with other physical security frameworks and depend on IT frameworks with Internet abilities. Three crucial parts of this kind of system are the sensor, control unit, and annunciator. Sensors distinguish invasion using various measures. The control unit gets the caution warning from the sensor and afterward actuates a quie*t al*ert, or the annunciator will create a warning (*e.g.*, in the form of a light or alarm).

Many detection systems are suggested by various authors to protect the system from intrusion. In the first scheme [10], the authors detail the assault resistance issue as a two-player, nonzero-sum, non-agreeable game between an assailant and a sensor. In the first stage, a non-helpful game between the assailant and sensor hub's suggestion highlights the work. By utilizing the game hypothesis structure, the game accomplishes Nash equilibrium for the two- aggressors and IDS. The second scheme is known as the interruption discovery structure. It is dependent on Markov Decision Process. The system consolidates a learning system. In the starting, IDS watches the framework and learns the conduct of the adversary, and attempts to choose which hub that needs insurance. If it ensures that the assailant is trying to assault, the assault is made ineffective. However, if an aggressor strikes an unexpected hub in comparison to the sensor device, then it becomes fruitful. The third scheme has the utilization of a natural measurement. Traffic load is measured, and IDS decides to secure the hub, which has the most elevated measure of traffic load. The work simulation has 20-200 cluster heads. Pentium III having CPU 1133 MHz usage collects the readings in the required environment.

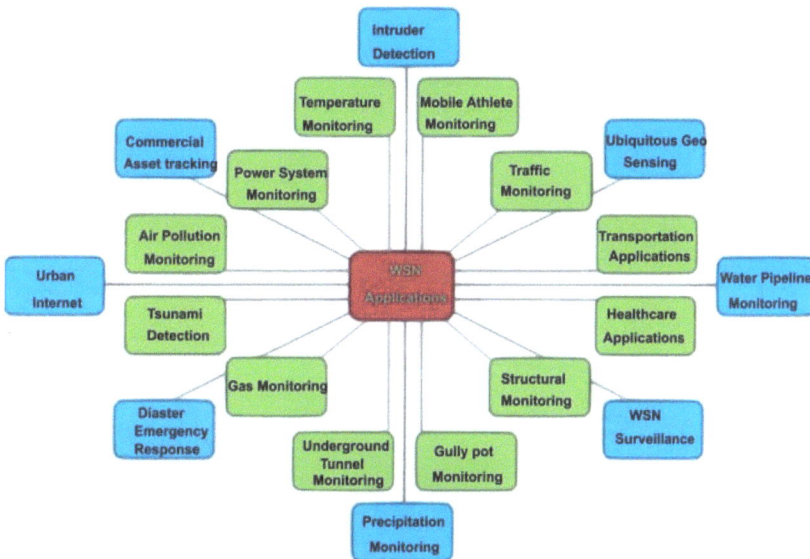

Fig. (1). Applications of wireless sensor network [9].

The interruption location framework [11] follows an appropriate design. It makes indistinguishable IDS customers running in every hub of the system. At that point, the IDS customers speak with one another to arrive at a resolution on an interruption occasion. Every customer follows a particular based methodology to recognize assaults. It distinguishes deviations from typical conduct given in the client characterized rules. The system director needs to differentiate and insert the bits by comparing each strike that the IDS ought to identify. Because of its nearsighted vision around its neighborhood, a hub will most likely be unable to settle on an executive choice. The proposal contains 100 randomly distributed nodes. It runs 1000 times to arrive at the watchdog with a unique ID. Mica2 (TinyOS) required 1.5KB of RAM and 3.9KB of ROM. The nodes are connected using MintRoute.

Ubiquitous Geo Sensing

Universal Geo-detection empowers the comprehension of the perplexing connections between aggregate human movement and climate designs. It can give bits of knowledge into essential procedures or cause-impact association. Some examples include instances of crisis supervisors who require time-basic choice help, open transportation administrators require the successful assignment of assets to upgrade the traffic stream, for project leads to help business insight.

One of the works [12] recognizes the impediments of existing impromptu based methodologies for preparing numerous total questions. It proposes emerged materialized in-network (MINVs) and related access procedures. The procedures include full scanning, replication cluster, and prefix sum.

GeoSENS [13] is a pairwise key foundation convention utilizing the zone data of the district in with sensor systems deployment. Dozens of utilization in a locale is considerably enormous than the sensor remote transmission territory with an overhead of putting away more keys in sensors.

Commercial Asset Tracking

Mechanized stock administration and resource tracking issues with traditional techniques include collecting, storing, and recovering data.

This procedure implementation is an enormous number of components in an organization, association, or foundation. A benefit portrayed by these systems is that they are remarkably identifiable. Some examples include framework depiction, physical area, or proprietor data. The advantage has a lot of recognizing attributes related to the defined identification number (series of numbers, characters, or a mix of both). As a couple, this information mapping (identification number and qualities) commonly goes into a database physically or utilizing a standardized tag framework.

The RFID framework and the remote sensor assembly have been coordinated in a study [14]. The commercial off-the-shelf (COTS) RFID framework gave various choices to coordinate with a remote sensor. The RS232 association fulfills the purpose of information, correspondence since the secluded sensor foundation offers a UART (Universal Asynchronous Receiver Transmitter) at a similar piece rate. The additional circuit acquaints with the interface. The UART of the remote sensor with the RS232 association of the RFID per user effectively changes over the transistor-transistor rationale (TTL) levels.

An Internet-connected RFID Sensor Network (iRfidSensorNet) framework [15] is created. It utilizes sensors, RFID labels, RFID perusers, smart-operator-bas-d-programming, remote and landline correspondence systems, and the Internet. It connects to Intranet, Extranet joins. These component assembly aids in ceaselessly distinguishing, detecting, checking, and conveying self-governing among the items bunched inside the RFID SensorNet's extended range. The iRfidSensorNet framework includes a majority of Wireless RFID/Sensor Tag Apparatus 200 for distinguishing, detecting, and estimating object conditions. The work uses an RFID Reader Apparatus 100 containing System Software 300. It is into a constant, simultaneous strategy to process component conditions and area data by giving an alarm to be transmitted to a remote observing station for consideration.

A SmartLOCUS framework [16] is an assortment of implanted stages. Every stage or device intends to follow its area. Every device knows when it is moving and when its position is steady. The stable instrument helps moving hubs and figure out where they are. Ordinarily, a couple of appliances called foundation hubs, are sent to the desire that they will rarely move. A different device is called portable devices and is required to move now and again including leaving a space and reappearing sometime in the future. It naturally discovers its neighbor hubs when another tool is in its capacity and, utilizing the data given by them, decides its area inside the space. SmartLOCUS uses the speed distinction of ultrasound (US) signal and a radio frequency (RF) sign to ascertain the movements between devices. A US signal spreads at the speed of sound (340 m/s). An RF signal proliferates at the speed of light (300,000,000 m/s).

Water Pipe Monitoring

Long pipelines are a part of numerous nations for various applications. For instance, a long duct moves water from desalination plants. These reside near the ocean, in urban communities that are a long way from the water bodies. In the Middle East, major cities like Riyadh, home to more than 4,000,000 individuals. They are dependent on the water moved through gigantic and long pipelines from the Shoaiba Desalination Plant in Al-Jubail in the eastern piece of Saudi Arabia.

Saudi Arabia is presently the world's biggest maker of desalinated water, providing major urban and modern regions through a system of water pipes that run for more than 3,800 km. A system requires a pipeline office for various applications. Instances of these applications are to take estimations inside or outside the pipelines. Inside estimations undergo weighted, streamed, and temperature estimation. Occurrences of outside estimators include pipeline region checking, pipeline assurance cameras, pipeline fire discovery, and pipeline fluid spillages.

The suggestion is Magnetic Induction (MI) based remote sensor organization for underground pipeline checking (MISE-PIPE) [17]. The system is acquainted with minimal effort and continuous monitoring over spillage location. MISE-PIPE recognizes and limits spillage by using the estimations of various kinds of sensors that are found both inside and around the underground pipelines. By embracing a MI waveguide system, the estimate of divergent sorts of sensors all through the pipeline system can be accounted for by the organization progressively. The data transmission of the MI waveguide is 1 kHz. The working recurrence is 10 MHz. The hand-off curls have a similar span of 0.15 m, and the quantity of turns is 20. The twine is copper wire with a 1.45 mm measurement. The expense and weight of curls made of this sort of wire are neglectable. The wire obstruction of unit length is 0.01 X/m.

PipeNet [18] is a framework dependent on the remote sensors organization that plans to identify, restrict, and evaluate blasts and spills and different inconsistencies in water transmission pipelines. The structure usage deals with observing water quality in transmission and checking the water level in sewer gatherers. The creators have structured a sensor board to interface the Intel Mote (comprising of an ARM7 Center, 64kB RAM, 512kB Flash, and Bluetooth radio) to different simple sensors utilized in PipeNet. The sensor block supports eight uncomplicated channels. The Analog-to-Digital Converter (ADC) association with a complicated programmable rationale gadget (CPLD) is answerable for driving the ADC clock. It accomplishes the ideal inspecting rate and crossing over the Serial Peripheral Interface (SPI) of the ADC to the Universal Asynchronous Receiver/Transmitter (UART) interface upheld by the bit.

Urban Internet

Urban natural surroundings are progressively inclined to obstruct isolated correspondence. The populace in urban territories is expanding step by step bringing about clog and commotion contamination. Mechanical arrangements focus on the least cost, low vitality utilization. WSN arrangement in an urban situation has picked up so much notoriety that various eccentric applications have prodded up from every road. Remote sensor systems convey in sewers for sewage flood checking, methane, and different dangerous gases observing in the sewerage. The procedure is an answer to the calamity alleviation procedure, foundation checking, and observation of crimes.

SenseMyCity (SMC) [19], and IOT versatile urban sensor is substantially configurable. The stage comprises an application, a back-office, and a front office. The SMC application can gather information from implanting sensors, similar to GPS, WiFi, accelerometer, magnetometer, and so forth. Information transmission to the servers can either on-request or progressively minimize expenses by utilizing the arranged kind of Internet. The creators are using Samsung I5500 running Android rendition 2.3.7 with a solitary center 600 MHz CPU and a 1200 mAh battery - to a 2012 incredible model - LG Nexus 4 E960 running Android 4.2.2 with a quad-Center 1.5 GHz CPU and a 2100 mAh battery. The examination required at any rate five runs of every design and cell phone model.

Precipitation Monitoring

The precipitation sensor incorporates an optical producer and reflects in visual correspondence with the optical producer. The prime mirror surface reflects and collimates light outflow from the ocular manufacturer. The second glass adjusts to the center aligns light upon the optical beneficiary. The precipitation sensor further remembers a middle of the road reflector for visual correspondence with the primary mirror Surface and with the Second mirrors Surface. Precipitation shows the little scope of changeability and profoundly non-normal fact conduct that requires a visit, firmly dispersed perceptions for adequate portrayal. Such illusions are impractical through surface-based estimations over a considerable part of the globe, especially in marine, remote, or in progressing places.

EUMETSAT [20] understood the Multi-sensor Precipitation Estimate (MPE) to consolidate the benefits of the high, fleeting, and similarly high spatial goals of a geostationary IR sensor with higher precision in the downpour rate recovery of microwave sensors on polar-circling satellites. IR-pictures from METEOSAT 7 on a geostationary circle at 0° longitude is co-situated with detached microwave information from the Special Sensor Microwave/Imager (SSM/I). The recovery of downpour rates from microwave information depends on built calculations. A measurement coordinating in fleet and land windows connection to the IR splendor temperatures recovers downpour rates. The size of the reality windows choosing fits the size of the run of the mill brief climate frameworks.

The Tropical Rainfall Measuring Mission (TRMM) and Multi-satellite Precipitation Analysis (TMPA) proceed with a pattern. It moves towards routine calculation and conveyance for better scale precipitation. The essential combination of microwave and infrared undergoes estimation performance at the 3-hourly, 0.25° scope longitude goals. Just the same as the GPCP items, the TMPA is intended to join precipitation gauges from different satellite frameworks. Similar to land-surface precipitation measures and examines the work activation takes place. Whenever the situation allows, the last item will have adjustment noticeable back to the single "best" satellite gauge. TMPA gauges creation happens in four phases. The microwave precipitation gauges are adjusted directing to consolidation, and infrared precipitation gauges use the aligned microwave precipitation. The microwave and IR gauges undergo joining, and downpour measure information is fused.

Health Applications

A wireless body sensor (BSN) [21] is an arrangement or an assortment of wearable sensors speaking with nearby nodes aiming to transmit the packets to the home gadget. The setting has massive potential for changing individual day by day lives. They can upgrade numerous human-focused application areas, for example, m-Health, m-game, and human-focused applications that include physical/virtual social co-operation.

The creators [22] have proposed signal handling in condition, an open-source programming structure, intended to help fast and adaptable prototyping and the board of BSN applications. SPINE offers help for dispersed sign handling significant BSN applications [23] by the immense arrangement of predefined physiological sensors. It acts as coordinator signal-preparing utilities, adaptable information transmission, and streamlined system/asset with the board. The creators [24] have proposed BSN engineering utilizing various remote biosensors includes 3-lead ECG, 2-lead ECG strip, and SpO2 sensors. The proposed delineates the most recent structure of the BSN nodes and their interoperability with other WSN stages, for example, MicaZ and Telos. Darwish and Hassanien (2011) [25] clarifies the significant job of body sensors organization in medication to limit the requirement for parental figures and help the constantly sick and old individuals carry on with an autonomous life, other than giving individuals' quality consideration. It is a far-reaching examination of the different advantages and downsides of these frameworks. The clothing contains sensors for ceaseless checking the welfare information and leading textures going about as cathodes to catch the body signals. The deliberate physiological electrocardiogram information and physical movement information are moved to an Adhoc arrange to utilize the IEEE 802.15.4 correspondence standard for base-stations and a server PC for remote checking. The system contains a wrist-worn wearable clinical check and ready frame focusing on high-chance cardiovascular/respiratory patients. It screens physiological boundaries, for example, electrocardiograms, pulse, circulatory strain, skin temperature, and so on.

The work [26] exhibits the improvement of a scaled-down telemetered wandering observing gadget in a ring arrangement. The device calls a ring sensor that is worn by the patient continuously. The welfare status observation update happens 24 hours per day. The ring outfitting with LEDs and photograph identifies heartbeat oximetry execution usage made for checking beat waves and blood oxygen immersion. The deliberate information is transmitted to a PC through an advanced remote correspondence connect, and the patient welfare status noting happens consistently and remotely. Any attribute of anomalous wellbeing status and potential mishaps identification happens by breaking down the sensor information.

Trung and Lee (2016) [27] discussed updated progress concerning sensor-integrated wearable stages in detail. The most recent accomplishments concerning self-powered sensor-integrated wearable stage innovations are part of the exploration. The recommendation [28] exhibits a circulated Telemonitoring framework. It is planned for improving human services, and helps to subordinate individuals in their homes. The framework executes a help situated engineering-based stage, which permits heterogeneous remote sensor systems to impart in a circulated manner autonomous of time and area confinements. The ZigBee gadgets cover the home of every patient to be checked. There is a ZigBee remote control conveyed by the verified patient that fuses a catch, compressing in the event of isolated help or critical assistance. Every one of these ZigBee hubs incorporates a C8051F121 microcontroller and a CC2420 IEEE 802.15.4 radio recurrence handset. Bluetooth device utilizes a BlueCore4-Ext chip with diminished guidance set PC (RISC) microcontroller with 48 KB of RAM and 1024 kB of external glimmer memory and is perfect with the Bluetooth 2.0 norm.

CareNet [29] is a multi-layered programming foundation dependent on the highlights and capacities of every one of the system levels. The framework Shift from a facility arranged, brought together human services framework to a patient-situated, and conveyed the medicinal services framework. It reduces corporal services costs by increasingly effective utilization of clinical assets and prior identification of ailments. The sensors can speak with the base station sensors legitimately utilizing IEEE 802.15.4 remote norm. Furnished with IEEE 802.11 isolated connectors, the spine switches communicate with one another and hand-off the development detecting information just as video streams to the home human services door.

Temperature Monitoring

Temperature checking hardware will assist you with avoiding heat development of your telecom areas, similar to cabins and other system hubs, by giving constant observing of the site. Temperature observing frameworks is likewise significant at less modern "IT" areas like server rooms and server farms. A focal temperature monitoring framework will empower you to monitor primary temperatures at all of your destinations that contain significant PC gear. A simple sensor is better than computerized sensors since it tracks temperature progressively over a nonstop range.

The work [30] is an inserted remote sensor arrange (WSN) model framework for temperature checking in a structure. This system will use for the administration of cooling frameworks at SIIT. A definitive objective is to help sparing vitality expenses and diminishing vitality utilization. The structure gives a web UI to any client to get to the present and past temperature readings in various rooms. The system comprises an information portal or facilitator which remotely surveys each WSN temperature-checking hub situated in every study hall. Each WSN hub is a microcontroller on the Arduino board, and an Xbee remote corresponding module depends on the IEEE 802.15.4/Zigbee models. The organizer additionally has an Ethernet interface and runs a primary information web server. Subsequently, the organizer permits information assortment over Xbee and information access from internet browsers.

A long-range UHF RF distinguishing proof (RFID) sensor has been planned [31] utilizes a 0.35-μm CMOS standard procedure. The force improved tag, joined with the ultra-low-power temperature sensor, permits an ID, and a temperature perusing scope of 2 m from a 2-W viable transmitted force yield power per user. The temperature sensor depends on a ring oscillator, where the temperature reliance of the wavering recurrence uses to warm detecting. The temperature sensor shows a goal of 0.035 °C and error esteem lower than 0.1 °C in the range from 35 °C to 45 °C after a two-point adjustment. The traditional power utilization of the temperature sensor is just 110 nW at ten changes for each second while keeping a high goal and precision. These properties permit the use of the RFID as a battery-less sensor in a remote human internal heat level observing framework.

Gas Monitoring

To improve individuals' solace, well being, and security screen Indoor Air Quality (IAQ) is part of the routine. Migraines, queasiness, unsteadiness, and throat disturbance are usual side effects of the purported Sick Building Syndrome (SBS).

Another significant undertaking in observing IAQ is the discovery of hazardous circumstances, similar to pipe spillage. CH4 (methane) is a vital constituent of the flammable gas utilized in pretty much every family unit for cooking or warming. At the point when it arrives at a specific focus in the air (5-15%), it is combustible and touchy. CO (carbon monoxide) sources are tobacco smoke, gas warmers, and stoves, spilling smokestacks, and so forth. It is dull, scentless, boring, and subsequently tough to see without a detecting gadget. In smaller amounts causes migraines and discombobulation following two or three hours of introduction. Higher focuses cause cerebral pains and tipsiness after 5-10 min and passing inside 30 min. High fixations cause obviousness after two or three breaths, trailed by death in under 3 min.

The device is planned [32] with low rest flow utilization (just 8 μA), and it contains a metal-oxide-semiconductor gas sensor and a pyroelectric infrared (PIR) sensor. Moreover, the system is multimodal. It abuses data from helper sensors, for example, PIR sensors about the nearness of individuals and from the neighbor hubs about gas fixation to change the conduct of the device and the estimating recurrence of the gas focus. The proposal comprises of a few sensor hubs sorted out as IEEE 802.15.4/ZigBee organize, group tree design. The primary device is the ZigBee organizer, and the end gadgets are associated with the switches in a star-like way. The hub works around the Jennic JN5148 module. It is an ultra-low-power, superior remote microcontroller focused on ZigBee PRO systems administration applications. The gadget includes an upgraded 32-piece RISC processor, a 2.4 GHz IEEE 802.15.4 compatible handset, 128 kB of ROM, 128 kB of RAM, and a blend of simple and advanced peripherals. Its capacity utilization is 15 mA for TX and 18 mA for RX.

The wireless gas sensor network (WGSN) [33] comprises of a sensor device, a transfer device, a system organizer, and a remote actuator. The sensor achieves early gas discovery utilizing a locally available 2D semiconductor sensor. Since the sensor devours a considerable measure of intensity, it contrarily influences the device lifetime, a heartbeat warming profile to accomplish huge vitality investment funds. The hand-off device gets and advances traffic from the sensor towards the system organizer and the other way around. At the point when a crisis is recognized, the system facilitator alerts an administrator through the GSM/GPRS or Ethernet organize and may self-sufficiently control the wellspring of gas outflow through the remote actuator.

Power System Monitoring

The power framework is immense because of the interconnections between each assistance territory to improve unwavering quality and financial productivity. The social structure has primarily dependent on electrical vitality for superior life and commercial development. Then again, the power framework is presented to the routine habitat consistently. The foundation has some, little, or enormous unsettling influences. Some instances include lightning, hurricane, and device deficiencies. Under these conditions, the framework should keep up stable activity to maintain a strategic distance from power outages in the entire frame utilizing proper assurance and control plans. In the interconnected foundation, there are a few challenges in assessing and keeping up the security of the whole framework.

The electrical force framework [34] encompasses sensor gadget incorporates sensor hardware designed to screen a trait of electrical vitality. It is an electrical channel of an electrical force framework, and connection arranged to situate the sensor hardware concerning the electrical conveyor. The sensor hardware screens the attribute of the electrical vitality led by an electrical transmitter of the electrical force framework. The sensor hardware is electrically secluded from the electrical antenna of the electrical force framework. In one exemplification, the ADCs 130 give 14 bits of testing goals to cover the current scope of 0 to 5,000 Amperes with a sum of +/ - 8,192 goals with 1 Ampere gradual qualities. For SCADA applications, ADCs 130 give 16 piece tests at 128 examples usage. ADCs 130 gives eight ksps and making some transformation memories of fewer than ten us in one embodiment. Electrical vitality is regularly disseminated and transmitted at 50 or 60 Hz AC in a model force conveyance or transmission execution. A cycle is roughly 20 ms for a total sine wave of 50 HZ vitality.

There are two particular divisions inside the framework [35]. The parts to one side of the transport are slave segments, and the other is ace segments. The framework transport has three divisions - information, intrude, and power control. The slaves invade on deliver belt utilizing concentrated discretion if more than one slave has a hinder flag. The slaves additionally react to peruse or compose demands from the ace side on the information transport. The engineering interfaces with the low-power CC2420 802.15.4 radio from ChipCon. It includes a 2-kilobyte custom on-chip SRAM. It expends 2.07 µW while working at 100 kHz and 1.2V. The clocking subsystem comprises of a lot of four 16-piece clocks in usage. The message processor model handles standard 802.15.4 parcels.

The vitality coupler [36] changes over the collected air conditioning, power into Direct Current (DC) utilizing detached voltage multiplier circuit. The plan of the vitality coupler is with the end goal that the DC power is sufficient to charge a smaller than typical 1.2-V battery-powered battery. It is the vitality coupler equipped for conveying ten mW of DC capacity to a 50-ohm load.

Air Pollution Monitoring

Transport significantly affects the earth, wherein we live. It partitions into four headings- nearby air quality, environmental change, clamor, and waterway contamination. The clean air [37] is fundamental to human wellbeing. The Environment Agency assesses that traffic sources represent over 97% of Carbon Monoxide (CO) and 75% of Nitrogen Oxides (NOX) emanations. Other striking commitments contain the traces from mechanical plant and premises, household vitality creation, and development action in any dirtied zone. To screen the poisons detecting group examines their consequences for the earth. It gathers continuous contamination information on relevant parts of traffic conditions, discharges, and encompassing toxin focus. The objective is to build up the capacity to quantify, display, and anticipate the scope of natural contaminations and risks utilizing a framework of the unavoidable side of the road.

Air contamination is a blend of sturdy particles and gases noticeable. Vehicle discharges, synthetic concoctions from industrial facilities, residue, and dust suspension aggregate the issue. At the point when ozone structures air contamination, it is called brown haze. Some air toxins are noxious. Breathing in them can expand the opportunity to cause medical issues. Individuals with heart or lung complaints are at more hazards from air contamination. Air contamination is the air inside structures that can likewise be dirtied and influence human wellbeing.

Wireless Sensor Network Air Pollution Monitoring System (WAPMS) [38] is screen air contamination in Mauritius using remote sensors. It sends the readings in large numbers around the island. The proposed framework utilizes an Air Quality Index (AQI). To improve the effectiveness of WAPMS, the authors have planned and executed another information accumulation calculation named Recursive Converging Quartiles (RCQ). The calculation usage blends information to kill copies, sift through invalid readings and outline them into a more straightforward structure. The methodology decreases the measure of data to be transmitted to the sink and along these lines sparing vitality. The executives have utilized various leveled directing conventions in WAPMS and made the bits rest during the stationary time.

The proposed framework comprises a Mobile Data-Acquisition Unit (Mobile-DAQ) and a fixed Internet-Enabled Pollution Monitoring Server [39]. The Mobile-DAQ unit coordinates remote chip microcontroller, air contamination sensors, a General Packet Radio Service Modem (GPRS-Modem), and a Global Positioning System Module (GPS-Module). The Pollution-Server is of good quality PC application server with Internet availability. The Mobile-DAQ unit assembles air toxin levels (CO, NO_2, and SO_2) and packs them in a casing with the GPS physical area, time, and date. The case is in this manner transferred to the GPRS-Modem and transmitted to the Pollution-Server through the versatile system. A database server joins the Pollution-Server for putting away the toxin level for additional utilization by different customers. Some of the examples contain ecological assurance offices, vehicle enlistment specialists, and insurance agencies. The Pollution-Server interfaces with Google Maps to show ongoing contamination levels and areas in metropolitan regions. The frame effects in the city of Sharjah, UAE. The microcontroller is a solitary chip gadget that has advanced yield ports, 16 channels, 8/10 bits simple-to-computerized converter, eight interfere driven clocks, 12K bytes of RAM, 4K bytes of EEPROM, 256K bytes of EEPROM, two RS-232 sequential correspondence ports, 4 Control Area Network ports, and SPI correspondence ports. The sensor cluster comprises three air contamination sensors, including Carbon Monoxide (CO), Nitrogen Dioxide (NO_2), and Sulphur Dioxide (SO_2). Every one of the above sensors has a straight current yield in the scope of 4 mA-20 mA. The four mA yield compares to zero-level gas, and the 20 mA relates to the most extreme gas level. A primary sign molding circuit intended to change over the four mA-20 mA goes into 0-5 V to be well with the voltage scope of the inherent simple-to-computerized converted in the 16-piece single-chip microcontroller. The general bundle radio assistance (GPRS) is a parcel situated versatile information administration utilized in 2G and 3G cell corresponding frameworks worldwide framework for portable interchanges (GSM).

Tsunami Detection

A tsunami is a progression of waves produced when earth plate limits suddenly and vertically uproot the overlying water. A few out of every odd tremor creates a tidal wave. Adrift usage resolves the issue. A tidal wave has a lot of littler wave stature seaward with lengthy frequency. This wave goes at a speed of more than 800 km/h. Because of the tremendous recurrence, the ripple has a frequent abundance of less than 1 m. It makes tidal waves hard to recognize the strident water supply. As the tidal wave moves toward the coast and the water gets shallow. It compacts because of ripple shoaling, and it speeds eases back down to 80 km/h. Its frequency reduces to less than 20 km, and its sufficiency develops tremendously, delivering an unmistakably noticeable wave. Tide checks conveyance at the coast usage for tidal wave waveform chronicles. These measures utilization watches torrents a long way from perception locales.

The proposed approach [40] can recognize the changes in pictures of enormous size, though the augmentation of the changing zone is small. The technique depends on the accompanying a split of the large size picture into sub-pictures. A versatile investigation on them is a programmed split-based limit choice methodology. This general methodology utilization characterizes a framework for harm appraisal in multitemporal synthetic aperture radar (SAR) pictures. The proposed framework appropriately recognizes various degrees of harms that are instigated by tidal waves alongside beachfront regions.

The work [41] depicts the reenactment of wave related marks measured by HF radar at extended ranges (if there should be an occurrence of a tidal wave going towards the coast). The HF radar framework WERA is oceanographic radar set on the coastline, and it gives concurrent wide-zone estimations of sea surface flow fields and ocean state parameters. A wave occasion is displayed utilizing the oceanographic HAMburg Shelf Ocean Model (HAMSOM), which has high spatial and fleeting goals and gives the sea surface flows instigated by moving toward the wave. The tidal wave current speed is changed over into regulating signals and superimposed on estimated receiving wire signs of the WERA radar. The conceivable sea surface and flow changes because of a tidal wave occasion assessment utilize a quick update of the radar backscattered spectra. The proposal is a torrent discovery strategy depends on the arranged insights consistent bogus alert rate (CFAR) identification, calculation applied to the entropy recorded of surface flows. It offers a chance to give a mechanized tidal wave alert during the ongoing observation by the WERA radar.

Soil Monitoring

Environment observing has been a significant piece of Wireless Sensor Network Applications. It develops broadly alongside the advancement of ongoing innovation. By and large, natural observing framework controls and screens condition parameters, for example, temperature, dampness, light, and weight. Remote sensor arranges innovation permits constant soil, water content checking with a high spatial and worldly resolve on for watching hydrological forms in little watersheds. The isolated sensor organization is an innovation that gives the ideal and incorporated answers for disseminating information collection, delivery, and examination in farmland. An infield soil dampness and temperature checking framework created meets the application necessity in the farmland environment.

The work [42] assesses a minimal effort soil and water content sensor facility. The field test includes a correlation of water content estimations of a woods soil at 5 cm profundity utilizing TDR and EC-5 sensors. The work [43] depicts the plan and usage of responsive, occasion-driven systems for natural observing of soil dampness and assesses its adequacy. The recommendation is the structure and trial of a sensor arrangement that effectively meets the objective of reactivity. It exhibits palatable power and system lifetime. Field preliminaries show the reactivity, strength, and life span of the system are displayed and assessed. The dirt dampness sensor organizes tried at Pinjar utilizes Mica2 bits with MDA300 sensor sheets and Echo20 soil dampness tests. The Superlite is a remote board PC containing a Sony Ericsson GSM module. It is associated with the sensor arrange by appending the base hub to a MIB510 programming board. It afterward interfaces the programming board to the Superlite utilizing a hybrid sequential link. The Superlite, along with the versatile observing premise, goes about as an indirect association between the sensor arrange and an online database. Once in the database, the TinyOS messages can be recovered and decoded utilizing an uncommonly devised SOAP-based web administration. GPRS associates the Superlitewith the Internet.

The examination [44] was to research the capability of remote sensors to arrange innovation for the constant observing of soil, water content (SWC) at the field, and headwater catchment scale utilization of creating remote sensor organizations SoilNet. The minimal effort permits innovation transmission in remote control and checking applications. ZigBee is a setup of elevated level correspondence conventions that utilizes little, low-power digital radios dependent on the IEEE 802.15.4 standard for scheduled individual region networks. The bit of the correspondence equipment is the ZigBee-consistent, high-power, remote module JN5139. It utilizes the unlicensed 2.4-GHz band and supports star, tree, and straight geographies.

A mechanized water system framework [45] creation streamlines water use for horticultural yields. The frame has a disseminated remote system of soil-dampness and temperature sensors set in the root zone of the plants. A portal unit handles sensor data, triggers actuators, and also transmits information to a web application. A calculation created with edge estimations of temperature and soil dampness was customized into a microcontroller-based entryway to control the water amount. The framework checks the photovoltaic boards and has a duplex correspondence connect dependent on a cell Internet interface that considers information, examination, and water system planning modification through a website page. WSUs convey in-field to arrange a dispersed sensor organize for the robotized water system framework. Every unit depends on the microcontroller PIC24FJ64GB004 that controls the radio modem XBee Pro S2 and procedures data from the dirt dampness sensor (VH400) and the temperature sensor DS1822. The battery-powered AA 2000-mAh Ni-MH Cycle Energy batteries fuels it. The photovoltaic board MPT4.8-75 holds the charge.

The solar oriented fuel framework [46] acknowledged the ongoing checking and recording of soil dampness data that gave information supports to additionally water-sparing water system methodology arrangement. The recommendation considers [47] WSN with the GIS arrangement of the dirt dampness appropriation guide. Utilizing the setup dampness conveyance guide of the dirt is read. The work uses MICAz type modules. These modules take a shot at the worldwide 2.4 GHz ISM band with help from IEEE802.15.4/ZigBee. All modules incorporate a completely programmable microcontroller, a two-way ISM band radio handset, and memory for over-the-air-programming and information logging of up to 100,000 estimations. The proposal uses a VGA-400 soil dampness sensor.

A controllable water system framework [48] coordination shuts circularity control. It conveys to a remote in-field sensor arrangement for the robotized variable-rate water system. A test field was divided into five soil zones depending on the soil's electrical conductivity. The dirt, water sensors were adjusted with a neutron test and independently recognized for their reaction ranges at each zone. Water system choices were set-explicitly made dependent on criticism of soil, water conditions from circulating infield sensor stations. The water system control framework was executed and tried on a test field at the USDA-ARS-Northern Plains Agricultural Research Laboratory in Sidney, Mont. The 1.5-ha field spreads out in 15 strips toward movement. Each one plans to malt grain. It is an aggregate of 90 individual plots of 15 m wide and 9m long. Each strip separates into six landscapes. Four catch jars were introduced in each dirt zone and adjusted between two MESA sprinkler heads, separated three is separated, and 0.8 m over the ground. Five arrangements of catch jars introduced over a strip contain each of the five soil zones.

Remote sensor arrangement [49] is farming with low information rate applications. This system incorporates a sun-based fuel obtaining stations utilized on soil dampness estimations in nurseries and open field crops to improve water system proficiency. Soil dampness detection uses the two test heat-beat strategy.

An examination [50] was intended to assess the concurrent warmth and water (SHAW) model by contrasting its dirt, water expectations, and estimated soil water substance gathered by electrical opposition sensors during the Monsoon '90 multidisciplinary field analysis. The sensors gather hourly soil, water estimations in shrub-dominated destinations with enormous uncovered interspaced territories. Information assembled by the sensors undergoes adjustment for time, area Reflectometer, and the sensor estimations water set nearby the electrical opposition sensors utilizing an *in situ* alignment procedure.

The framework [51] comprises the dirt, observing the remote sensor system, and isolated information center. In the sensor network, the sensor assembly uses the JN5121 module, an IEEE 802.15.4/Zigbee secluded microcontroller. The sink nodes for accumulating and delivering system information depend on the ARM9 processor stage to meet the necessities of high-performance. A GPRS module coordinates into the sink node for long separation correspondence. The plausibility of using usually accessible earthbound WSN equipment arrangements in the underground condition is analyzed [52].

Habitat Surveillance

Today, thickly made sensor systems are being scaled to the size of the living beings under investigation, testing marvels at frequencies the life forms experience, and scattered in designs. These designs catch the full scope of ecological exposures to give the fine-grain data required for exact demonstrating and forecast. Natural surroundings observing applications comprise of different programming parts actualizing center framework administrations.

The approach [53] usage indicates and conveys information about intrigue. It needs a directing and entrusting administration. The creator's [54] research is deteriorating and coordinated effort in a two-layered sensor organization for observing. The frame perceives and restricts a predefined sort of bird calls. It has a couple of amazing macro-nodes at the primary level and a lot less incredible micro-nodes at the subsequent level. The examination consists of two kinds of lightweight preprocessing. It decreases information transmission from micro-nodes to macros-nodes.

INSIGHT (Internet Sensor InteGration for HabitaT observing) is research to lifetime, remote questioning and design, simplicity of arrangement, and unwavering quality. The "delta revealing" procedure utilized empowers both quick response time to changes in sensor readings. The system can accomplish around a half year lifetime by inspecting sensors consistently.

The creators [56] portray the plan and organization of WSN to screen seabirds on Skomer Island, a UK National Nature Reserve. The work outlines the advancement of the framework over a time of three years. Tovar, Friesen, Ferens, & McLeod (Tovar, Friesen, Ferens, & McLeod, 2010) writes about a starter investigation of applying isolated sensor organization utilizing DTN (Delay Tolerant Network) to test the present status of a specific untamed life well-evolved creature with the name of White Tail Deer in the WMU Area 47 Ontario, Canada North of Parry Sound District. The status of whitetail deer and identify different sorts of creatures are collected.

The creators [57] present a web interface model for natural surroundings, checking to utilize remote sensor arrangement used for innumerable uses. The interface created gives a user-friendly situation and a lot of functionalities that ease the collaboration between the end-clients and the WSN. The web interface portrays with particularity, which makes applications effectively extensible.

Disaster Emergency Response

The sensor organizes, captures data, processes, and correspondence the respective information for use by first responders. Sensor systems comprise of low-power and minimal effort gadgets with constrained computational and remote correspondence capacities. They speak to the following isolated correspondent by scaling down their power and size. It makes it practical to implant them into wearable crucial sign screens, area following labels in structures, and the person on call. It will know to screen and manage countless loss information is vital in debacle reaction situations. If specialists on-call cannot quickly triage the harmed and seriousness of the situation in a planned way [58], the enormous numbers could rapidly overpower crisis field faculty and clinical staff. It will keep them from giving quality injury care. Integrating a scope of remote gadgets with changing abilities into restorative, fiasco reaction, and crisis care situations raises new difficulties for the gadgets' interoperation.

The proposal [59] suggests to quantify different essential physiological wellbeing parameters - ECG and internal heat level of patients and older people, wellbeing status remotely in the ad-hoc organization, to the remote base station which is associated with an emergency clinic's principle. Li, *et al*, (2011) [60] proposed a proficient Emergency Rescue Navigation technique (ERN) by treating WSNs as route foundation. The methodology considers both passerby clog and salvages power adaptability. Mortal development consideration as system streams on the chart is the part of work. By figuring of the highest surge and least cut on the diagram, the framework can give firefighters salvage directions to wipe out primary risky territories, which may altogether diminish the clog and spare caught individuals.

Liu, *et al*, (2018) [61] suggest adjustable duty cycle-based fast disseminate (ADCFD) for the most transmission communication in the smart remote programming arrangement. In an ADCFD proposal, the obligation cycle of nodes acclimation gets program codes opportune. Along these lines, the transmission times and crisis transmission delays decrease.

Congestion-Adaptive and small stretch crisis Navigation (CANS) [62] suggestion use a level set strategy to follow the development of the exit and the limit of the unsafe territory. It works with the goal that individuals close by the dangerous region accomplish a gentle clog at the expense of a slightly alternate route. The individuals far off from the risk dodge superfluous take temporary re-routes. The system considers the circumstance in case of crisis elements by joining a neighborhood yet straightforward status refreshing plan. The system is the first WSN-helped crisis route calculation accomplishing both non-harsh clog and small stretch, where all tasks are in-situ completed with digital-physical collaborations among individuals and sensors. The system does not require area data or the dependence on a specific correspondence model. It is additionally circulated and versatile to the size of the system with restricted stockpiling on every device.

The proposal [63] includes volcanic information assortment that depends on activated location and information recovery to meet information quality requests. The investigations in northern Ecuador led to Volcán Reventador. Tseng, *et al*, (2006) [64] have proposed a circulated route calculation for crisis circumstances. At ordinary times, sensors screen the earth. At the point when the sensors identify crisis occasions, the convention rapidly isolates risky zones from safe zones, and the sensors set up escape ways. The work [65] exhibits the practicality of utilizing financially intelligent, adaptable, and versatile sensor systems to address primary bottlenecks of the crisis reaction process. The miTag is a profoundly extensible stage that supports an assortment of sensors, additional items - GPS, beat oximetry, pulse, temperature, ECG, and transfers information over self-sorting out remote work arrangements. The pilot arrangements have become a significant patient checking assembly. Fulford-Jones *et al*, (2004) [66] have suggested Code Blue, a remote framework planned for the organization in crisis repair consideration, coordinating low-control, remote indispensable sign sensors, PDAs, and PC-class frameworks. Code Blue will upgrade specialists on the call's capacity to survey patients on scene, guarantees the consistent exchange of information among parental figures, and encourage productive allotment of emergency clinic assets.

Structural Monitoring

Barnes *et al*, (2007) [67] introduce a conveyed calculation to guide evacuees to exits through discretion complex structure designs in crisis circumstances. The computation finds the most secure ways for evacuees considering forecasts of the overall developments of dangers. Pan, Tsai, and Tseng [64] propose a novel 3D crisis administration that plans to direct individuals to safe spots when a crisis occurs. A typical time, the system is answerable for observing the earth. At the point when the calamity occurs, occasions are distinguished. The system can adaptively alter its topology to guarantee transportation dependability. It rapidly identifies hazardous locales that need maintenance from a strategic distance and discovers safe roadways that can lead individuals.

Tseng *et al*, (2006) [68] proposed a route calculation that underlines securely controlling individuals to escape from risky region. The structure permits numerous ways out and different crisis occasions in the detecting field. At ordinary times, sensors are answerable for checking the earth. At the point when crisis occasions are distinguished, the convention can rapidly recognize risky territories, and sensors can build-up escape ways that are as protected. ER-MAC [69] is a hybrid MAC convention for crisis reaction remote sensor systems. ERMAC is a hybrid structure of the Time-division multiple accesses (TDMA). It uses Carrier Sense Multiple Access (CSMA) approaches, giving it the adaptability to adjust to traffic and topology changes. It receives a TDMA way to deal with the plan impact-free spaces. Hubs wake up from their planned situate and switch into control sparing rest mode. At the point when a crisis happens, nodes that take an interest in the critical observing change their MAC conduct by permitting dispute in TDMA openings to accomplish high conveyance proportion and low inertness. ER-MAC offers a synchronized and free space structure to enable sensors to join or leave the system. Tabirca *et al*, (2009) [70] suggest a powerful model for the fire crisis clearing issue. The two potential situations portray using the dynamic model with a Wireless Sensor Network for fire crisis departure. The work actualizes using C++, and its execution utilized a standard PC machine with a Pentium 2.0 MHz processor and a RAM of 2.5 GB. The contribution is a model dependent on the ground floor of the UCC Environmental Research Institute building. This current floor's rooms and halls demonstrate with 35 hubs and 39 circular segments for the route chart. The route loads were produced by thinking about the physical separation between two devices and the slowest time an individual can navigate the circular segment.

Zeng *et al*, (2010) [71] suggest a crisis versatile, continuous, and robust directing convention for crisis circumstances. The accord adjusts to deal with dynamic catastrophe and functions admirably with the directing gap issue. The suggested framework [72] achieved the wise-database, which produces equipped messages to the handheld terminal by methods for the fire and air-based sensor information. The robot stage is arranging based versatility work for portable scrutiny. The creators used sensor modules with the CC2420 of TI Chipcon item as the RF handset and the ATMega128L as a principal processor. For arrange association, they have utilized one organizer hub, eight switches, 50 sensor hubs, and set tree-based system geography with a limit of 3 bounces. The remote radio transmission is 30-40 m, and the RF power control is 0 to −20 dBm. In the analyses, the length of the information bundle is 40 bytes, and the obligation cycle is 100%.

Boukerche *et al*, (2006) [73] suggest QoS-Aware Routing Protocol (QARP), a QoS-aware steering convention with administration separation for WASNs. The worldview utilization advances the connection among the sensors, on-screen quality nodes, and the sink. The QARP gives moderate dormancy and vigorous conveyance disappointments.

Traffic Monitoring

The goal of street traffic checking is to gather data about various traffic members. This data is vital to offer different types of assistance that empowers smoother, more secure, and ecologically cordial transportation. Instances of such administrations are versatile traffic signals, variable speed limits, voyager data, and course direction. One of the most significant traffic observing undertakings is the location of vehicles and walkers. If there should be an occurrence of prototypical traffic checking frameworks, this undertaking performed utilizes invasion identifiers in the asphalt roads. The establishment and upkeep of the ordinary finders are costly and incite genuinely interrupted by traffic.

The system [73] is a versatile traffic crossing point framework dependent on Wireless Sensor Network. The traffic light on one crossing point can speak with the traffic light of the following neighboring connexion, and traffic freedom organization for strange vehicles with the assistance of sensors. Based on the functionalities and drawbacks faced by the sensors, the work conducts SWOT analysis.

The area of the vehicle in the picture [74] changes into the vehicle's position and direction in real-time. The deformable vehicle model permits the vehicle's chief measurements to be estimated. This information might be passed to a significant level following calculation to remove traffic parameters, for example, vehicle momentum and intersection passage/leave measurements. The chief measure utilizes the arrangement of the vehicle inside classifications, for example, vehicle, van, or bus. The framework could likewise use it as a bootstrap procedure for quicker and sturdy calculations. The framework consists of a camera set up to screen vehicles arranging a T-intersection. It is at a stature of 8m over the street surface, slanted at an edge of 27.5 degrees under a flat plane corresponding to the street. Two vehicles arranging the intersection were then recorded on record and along these lines digitized at a pace of 3.77 casings/s and written to circle, giving one grouping of 36 edges in case of group A and one of 46 casings in case of group B.

The work considers the idea of Spatio-worldly connections in an urban traffic gridlock situation [75]. A class of scattering calculations that endeavor to loosened up client prerequisites for information precision to lessen the correspondence cost is adopted. The computation uses a reason for examination, proliferate the Fourier coefficients that establish the compacted adaptation of a device time arrangement to the nearest passage through the briefest way. Every device recognizes the minimal number of Fourier coefficients that remakes the time arrange, without playing out any further in-organize decrease. Execution assessment has been completed in Shanghai [76] by using the vehicle-based sensors introduced in around 4000 maneuvers. Two sorts of traffic status-estimation calculations, *i.e.*, the connection based and the vehicle-based, are presented and broke down. In assessing the nature of an excursion, drivers will, in general, consider the mean speed more than the stream rate or thickness. The mean speed has a presentation metric.

Gully Pot Monitoring

A minimal effort contribution made towards organizing a correspondence framework [77] contains planning, creation, and execution to give a sufficient admonition on potential blockage episodes to forestall sewer management. By observing the water level of the chasm pot, the water organization can be proactively educated regarding the best game-plan to take out the causal issue. Examples include blockage and spillage inside the sewer foundation. Consequently, the quantity of private sewer flooding and contamination episodes diminishes gradually.

The point of the examination [78] was to exhibit that water level information gathered at crevasse pots utilization decreases personal flooding episodes. The framework intends to screen the water level in gorge pots associated with the sewer arrangement. Zigbee based short-extended WSN chosen has a low information rate. It also supports inexpensive force utilization, straightforward correspondence framework, reasonable idleness, and capacity to help one ace and up to 65000 slave control units. The frame comprises of sensor hubs, an information finder, and a remote client terminal. Every instrument contains a radio handset, data securing board, and an acoustic detecting test. Correspondence between them performs by employing the Zigbee convention. The information finder speaks with the remote client terminal through either the Ethernet association or WiFi/GPRS. The primary technique uses a reverberation sounder that measures the time between the start of a beat of sound and the return of the resonance. The second technique is to assess the degree of signal quality received when the transmitter and recipient are either both submerged or noticeable all around.

To decide the pressure-driven and isolates execution of the manifolds, estimations with disseminated temperature detecting (DTS) have been completed [79] in both the foul sewer and the tempest sewer in the Bernhardsingel, Breda. The sewer arrangement of the Bernhardsingel includes a tempest sewer and a foul sewer.

Every 46 houses associations outfits with stormwater isolating complex. The sort of complex introduced per house association is obscure. The tempest sewer has a length of 382 m, with distances across running from 250 to 500 mm. The tempest sewer releases street overflow from ravine pots (0.37 ha) and rooftop spillover from manifolds (0.26 ha) legitimately through a Storm Sewer Outfall to getting water. The PVC foul sewer has a length of 381 m with a measurement of 200 mm. The sewer is associated with a siphoning station with a limit of 0.5 m³/h. Its limitation is adequate to release the typically dry weather flow of the 118 occupants. The observing set up includes a HALO SENTINEL PC associated with a fiber optic link of 850 m length. The HALO PC is situated in a compartment and put on a sewer vent. The underground level is a 40 mm association that has been made between the tempest sewer and the foul sewer to move the link from the foul sewer into the tempest sewer. To precisely find the link in it, high temp water has been released from a big hauler in it in extreme areas. The time goals applied is1 min, the spatial goals 2 m, and the relative exactness somewhere in the range of 0.1 and 0.2 W degrees centigrade.

Mobile Athlete Monitoring

Ongoing data on competitor pulse, temperature, speed, position, and effect during a live game can help recognize conceivably hazardous circumstances. For example, when a player's pulse or the temperature gets higher or when high weariness levels influence the body's physiological and bio-mechanical procedures to cause injury. Deliberately, ongoing data in field sports can help the mentor in improving group execution by making increasingly educated player replacement choices. Physiological and different sensors require some interchanging interface to encourage their planned capacity. The idea of the interface shifts broadly relies upon the kind of device just as its planned application. The use of a sensor stage extraordinarily disentangles the way of estimating an occasion and transforming it into something valuable by bestowing support for the device, preliminary sign molding, stockpiling information transmission, and application-explicit handling of the information. On account of wearing applications, this methodology permits fast framework customization and change. Along these lines, mapping with specialized aptitude, comprehension, and desires for sports researchers takes place. For instance, accelerometers utilization in such a framework has empowered the chronicle of competitor activity and capacity.

The methodology [80] permits us to bound that defers feasible by any useful plot and decides if constant information extraction is conceivable. The plausible sending plan transmits a message at each time moment until the example arrives at the base. The base can advise a player when its transmission is received, occurring each second. The execution would rely intensely upon the player position. The players found near a base will see a decent exhibition, rather than players situated in the focal point of the field. The disconnected ideal gives a proportion of the best reachable postponement. After the creation of an informal test, it undergoes transmission continuously in each space. When a neighbor gets a message, it is re-transmitted by the neighbor. The player's gadget at that point deletes its whole window of tests and the procedure re-begins. The outcomes in a flooding based approach deal with information spread.

The work [81] builds up an experimental model of the quality of the radio signal exuding from a competitor's body-worn gadget. The signal quality fluctuates with both angular direction and outspread separation when the transmitter the user wears against the body. Utilizing the experiment information, the creators infer a logical fit that gives a precise portrayal of the radio reach of a competitor's sensor gadget. This portrayal will permit producing the remote topologies emerging in the soccer field utilizing experiment information that tracks the area of players during the game. The method uses observational information to give a stochastic portrayal of preliminary parts of the dynamic remote topologies emerging during a soccer match. The authors have built a scientific model for creating dynamic topologies illustrative of authentic soccer matches. The contribution sets up availability that follows estimation in authorized games just as network information construed from the play area.

Underground Tunnel Monitoring

Condition checking in underground passages [82] is generally lengthy of many kilometers and widths of a few meters. It has been an urgent undertaking to guarantee safe working conditions in coal mineshafts where numerous natural components, including the measure of gas, water, and residue, need to be checked. To get full-scale checking of the passage condition examination information gathered at a wide range of spots. An exact situation review requires a high examining thickness, which includes countless detecting gadgets. Current strategies for coal mineshaft condition checking are commonly led scantily and manually because of the absence of methods for developing a programmed huge scope detecting framework. Using wires to associate detection focuses on the handling server. It requires a lot of wire arrangement, which is troublesome in case of poor working conditions and high upkeep costs underground.

Structure-Aware Self-Adaptive sensor framework (SASA) [83] utilizes a gap discovery calculation to screen the inward surface of passages by using radio signals among sensor hubs to show the structure of the sensor organization. With a suitable situation of sensor hubs and a cooperative component, SASA can precisely report areas of falls to identify and reconfigure dislodged hubs, therefore keeping up framework respectability. The equipment layer for our framework is the Mica2 mote stage created at UC Berkeley. The MPR400 radio board utilized has a 7.3 MHz microchip, with 128K bytes of program streak memory and 512K bytes of estimation streak memory. An 868/916 MHz tunable Chipcon CC1000 is a multi-channel handset with a 38.4 kbps transmitting rate usage for isolated correspondence with a 500-foot outside range.

WSN Surveillance

The classification of estimating methods for observation falls into two methodologies. The direct technique encompasses the estimation of the existent amount of the variable. Instances of it contain the utilization of cameras for visual review, radioactive isotopes, laser bars, and electrical obstruction in tool wear. The functional impediments address the issues during machining, light, and the utilization of cutting liquid. In any case, direct estimation has a high level of precision and its usage broadly to look into research centers. Indirect techniques are less exact than the other. The methodology undergoes testing to employ detecting gadgets to evaluate the procedure execution or to give data that process advancement utilizing sensors.

A reprogrammable observing and control framework [84] is for remote Sensors, and Subjects incorporates at least one versatile checking unit, every one of the convenient checking units having a Sensor, an area deciding gadget, and a Sensor interface unit. Every Sensor interface unit arrangement screens its Sensor and to transmit that Sensor's information, employing advanced remote correspondences organize, to a focal checking gadget. The versatile unit conveys or worn by an individual or creature or appended to a lifeless subject.

IoT-based Applications

Intelligent sensors [2] works as its parts convert this present reality variable that they are estimating into a digital information stream for transmission to a destination. The inherent microchip unit knowledge is made usage in different capacities. They aid in decreasing the heap on the IoT focal assets progressively. They can likewise detect any creation parameters that begin to float the past satisfactory standards and produce alerts in like manner. Some of the contributions based on their utilization summary fill the section below.

An IoT application [85] created for a particular functionality performs assigned tasks in the area. The sensors are embedded in these devices to accomplish the functionality. These devices perform their assigned tasks using the Internet. The devices will also be able to update their doings on the server or User-end. Some of the built-in structures that aid in the specific application detail in this section. Fig. (2) portrays IoT services and applications.

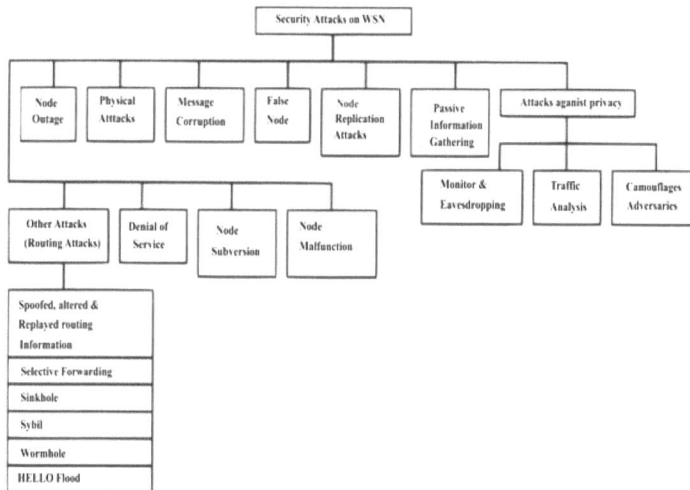

Fig. (2). Classification of security attacks in WSN [116].

The work [86] is the practical structure and execution of a total WSN stage. The methodology can be utilized for long haul natural checking its applications. The application provides ease, swift arrangement, long lifetime, low upkeep, and high caliber of administration. The hub microcontroller is an eight-piece ATMEL AVR ATtiny25 with 2 KB program and 128 bytes information memory, timed by its inward 8 MHz RC oscillator.

The work [87] design analyzes and restructures the IoT human services framework. The system screens the patient's welfare condition and aids in obtaining pertinent status parameters through a Web program whenever and wherever. It will increasingly verify social insurance applications and suitable on-time responses and measures. Patients who are not in typical condition are in consideration to shift from the medical clinic, and the observing of their essential parameters continuously can be performed from their homes. The work recreates utilizing the Cooja test system. Contiki 2.7 introduces on Ubuntu 14.04 OS. The stage chose for reenactment reasons for existing is Tmote Sky. It portrays by the accompanying: 8 MHz, 16-piece RISC processor with TI MSP430F1611 10 kB

RAM, 1 MB Flash memory, and Chipcon CC2420 handset at 2.4 GHz with transmission scope of around 100 meters. Medium Access Control (MAC) and physical layer characterize by IEEE 802.15.4 norm. The instrument utilized at the MAC layer is CSMA/CA. Radio Duty Cycle (RDC) instrument chose for recreation reasons for existing is the default worked in the Contiki system - ContikiMAC.

The structure of the framework [88] depends on the blend of unavoidable dispersed detecting units and data framework for information. The work delineates a successful minimal effort and adaptable answer for condition checking and vitality execution in home premises. The fundamental tasks incorporate remote administration and control of local gadgets, for example, electric light, water radiator, and so on. The inconspicuous checking of confined usages gives surrounding insight to decrease vitality utilization through IoT innovations are the key elements of the created framework. It will bolster and reschedule the occupant working time as per the vitality request and supply. The frame is the internetworking instruments, which are practicable to coordinate with co-modules like canny home checking frameworks for the health assurance of occupants. The ZigBee WSN involves XBee-S2 modules worked by Digi are arranged as end gadgets and impart remotely to an organizer as work geography. The organizer is associated with a switch with a wired sequential association. The handle runs an open-source implanted Linux (OpenWRT) programming, giving systems administration usefulness to interface the web. It provides web access to the Xbee-S2 sensor information gathered by the Xbee-S2 facilitator. The switch goes about as an IoT application passage and interconnects the IPv6 and ZigBee arrange. The work [89] is an accepted IoT approach for better wellbeing [90]. It is a control system of a person's welfare parameters like circulatory strain, hemoglobin count, glucose level, irregular cell development in any piece of the body, and so forth.

The work [91] is available on the CC2530 chip. It shows the structure and execution of farming Greenhouse Environment checking framework dependent on ZigBee innovation [92]. The remote sensor and control hubs take CC2530F256 as the center to control the information. This framework comprises of front-end information procurement, information preparation, information transmission, and information gathering. The encompassing temperature is always ready by the temperature sensor of the information terminal hub. Prepared information undergoes transfer to the middle of the channel device through a remote system. Halfway hub totals all information and afterward sends the information to the PC through a sequential port. Simultaneously, staff may view, examine. The framework embraces CC2530 produced by the T1 Corporation as the principle chip in the ZigBee correspondence module. A 2.4 GHz DSSS RF handset dependent on IEEE802.15.4 and a mechanical level low force, upgraded 8051 microchip center incorporates into a CC2530 single chip. The chip is power-sparing, with minimal effort. The data assortment module sensor uses the STM8S103F3 chip as a miniaturized scale processor.

Yang *et al.*, (2016) [93] have suggested a strategy for ECG checking [94] dependent on Internet-of-things (IoT) methods. ECG information is assembled utilizing a wearable observing hub and is transmitted legitimately to the IoT cloud uses Wi-Fi. Both the Hypertext Transfer Protocol (HTTP) [95] and Message Queuing Telemetry Transport (MQTT) conventions [96] are utilized in the IoT cloud to give visual and convenient ECG information to clients. The keen terminals with an internet browser can get ECG information.

The work [97] is an enhancement of continuous air contamination observation and determining the framework. It additionally displays the capacity of the gauging advancement pattern of air contamination inside a specific time. It undergoes an examination of the information by the front-end discernment framework, indicated by neural system innovation. Directed crisis transfer measures limit misfortunes in functional applications.

The recommendation [98] is to screen the condition of a photovoltaic framework through an IoT based system to control it remotely. The data from the sensors is transmitted employing the portable radio system. The test set up incorporates sun-based boards, temperature sensor LM35, voltage transducers, current transducers, SIM900A GPRS module, PIC18F46K22 microcontroller, RS232 interfaces, and converters. Programming Codes created in the house runs in MikroC programming, and hex code is stacked utilizing MPLAB programming. A GPRS module sends information to the remote server.

Mohanraj *et al*, (2016) [99] suggest an e-Agriculture Application dependent on the structure comprising of KM-Knowledge base and Monitoring modules. The system needs data all through the whole cultivating cycle to settle on the gainful alternative. The necessary data dispatching to different spots incorporates continuous data. Examples - advertising costs and current generation level details. An information-data flow model development interfaces with various dissipated sources to the yield structures. TI CC3200 Launchpad and Arduino UNO board with Ethernet Shield used to execute the checking modules. DHT11 Temperature and Humidity Sensor is part of the work. Soil Moisture Sensor (KG003), Ball skim fluid level Sensor, Magnetic Float Sensor for water level pointer fluid in the tank usage is part of the work. The Float sensor is an electromagnetic ON/OFF switch.BH1750 Module Digital Light force Sensor/LDR resistor. A Four Channel Relay Board (5V) for exchanging AC/DC employs to trigger an AC engine

(220V) to work the valves. L293D H Bridge (Wide Supply-Voltage Range: 4.5 V to 36 V) runs of the mill engine driver that permits the DC engine to drive on either course.

The gadget can be controlled and checked from a remote area [100] and implemented in agricultural fields, grain stores, and cold stores for security reasons. The work is situated to emphasize the strategies to take care of such issues as distinguishing proof of rodents, dangers to crops, and conveying continuous warning dependent on data investigation. The information sent from sensors to the Web server database utilizes remote transmission. In the server database, the data uses JSON design. The sensors and cameras are associated with the GPIO header. PIR sensor has three pins as VCC, OUT, and GND, while ultrasonic extending gadget (HC-SR04) contains four pins as TRIG, ECHO, VCC, and GND. The device has an ultrasonic sound-based rat repeller that will be actuated by a server-dependent on information investigation. Raspberry pi B+ GPIO header compromises of 40 pins that incorporate 5v, 3.3v, GND and 26 GPIO pins, and 2 ID-EEPROM pins to give network to I/O gadgets.

The water system [101] is computerized if the dampness and temperature of the field fall underneath the threshold. In nurseries, light force control can likewise be mechanized despite the water system. The warnings are sent to the system intermittently. The user can ready to screen the field conditions from anyplace. This framework will be progressively helpful in zones where water is rare.

The structure tries and is approved utilizing the ECG signals taken from the MIT-BIH arrhythmia and Physionet challenge databases [95]. The system supports continuous recording of ECG flag under various physical exercises.

Suma *et al*, (2017) [102] incorporates different highlights like GPS based remote controlled observing, dampness and temperature detecting, adversary detection, security, leaf wetness, and appropriate water system offices. It utilizes remote sensor systems for taking note of the dirt properties and natural factors consistently. Controlling these parameters are through any isolated gadget or internet providers. The tasks performance uses interfacing sensors, Wi-Fi, the camera with the microcontroller.

Mois *et al*, (2017) [103] suggest three different IoT-based remote sensors for ecological and surrounding checking. It utilizes User Datagram Protocol (UDP) [104] with Wi-Fi correspondence [105]. It conveys through Wi-Fi and Hypertext Transfer Protocol (HTTP), Bluetooth technology.

The system [106] is to screen air contamination on streets and track vehicles that cause infection over a predetermined point of confinement. The number of cars comprises set with an exceedingly lengthy time-span is considered. The work uses a mix of Wireless Sensor Network, Electrochemical Toxic Gas Sensors, and the utilization of a Radio Frequency Identification (RFID) labeling framework. It screens vehicle contamination records whenever anyplace. An Arduino board comprises of ATmega328 microcontroller permits to transfer new code without outer equipment software engineer and with corresponding segments to give offices like programming, joining into different circuits. A large portion of the loads up incorporates a 5-volt straight controller and clock speed of 16 MHz. The inputs used to interface several sensors or diverse equipment gadgets, a USB association utilized for speaking with the PC, another Arduino or different microcontrollers, and a reset button that permits it to reset by programming running on an associated PC without a physical press of the reset button. Info voltage provided to the board according to the proposal is 7 V to 12 V since the 5 V pin is under 5 V, and the board becomes insecure. If it is more than 12 V, the controller is overheating harm the board, and the DC per I/O pin ought to be 40 mAo. The board has a Flash memory of 32KB with 0.5 KB utilized for the bootloader, SRAM of 2 KB, and an EEPROM of 1 KB that can be perused or composed with EEPROM library. The Arduino UNO uses the Atmega 16U2 microcontroller customized as a USB-to-sequential converter. RFID has 14 digital input/yield pins, and six frequencies utilized for correspondence rely on, and range from 125 KHz to 2.45 GHz.

In the system [107] is used in assessing the advancements of home human services. It is improving this circumstance by helping the booked to remember prescription, remote observing, and update new drug information of patients (which should be possible by prescriber through the web). The information gathered helps the device of the Patient Prescription Drug Plans dependent on a patient's circumstance and inclinations. The instrument will give express data that will help the patient in deciding the most reasonable doctor prescribed medication plan, considering the individual significance of plan highlights. Using examine information on prescriptions of past patients who have a comparable welfare profile mapping to the present patient highlights the work.

The suggestion [108] comprises detecting units that see the ecological worth. Some examples include Humidity, temperature, heat record, gas, and so forth. It is additionally adjusted by the controlling framework to yield the accumulated information lastly gathered on the Internet-based stage. The system of associating the smart sensor to the Internet is accomplished by an IoT stage called Xively, which gives channel utility to convey the model into an incorporated item.

The work [109] is an electronic IoT arrangement planned for checking, following, and examining information in the farming territory. A piece of continuous information obtained is intermediary based distributing/buying in the Message Queue Telemetry Transport convention. Gathered data from sensors are put away on the web. Engineering of the web application portrayed as a customer server three-level design is the graphical User Interface (introduction layer), application capacities and rationale (application layer), and PC information stockpiling (database layer)created and kept up as autonomous modules, on independent stages. A model of the proposed framework actualizes in a tobacco drying furnace type SD - 78/2 (7270mm x 3150mm x 2850mm) with two chambers and coordinated wood consuming oven TD - 80. For the starting test, the system uses RaspberryPi model 3. Primary contrasts between RPi model 3 and earlier forms are incorporated remote module (802.11n), coordinated Bluetooth module (Bluetooth 4.1), and 1.2GHz 64-piece quad-center ARMv8 CPU. Utilizing this kind of RPi there is no requirement for extra modules for associating end gadgets to the system. Employing 1602A LCD screen appends to the control board, temperature, and mugginess esteems are appeared on the board.

The structure [110] applies to other portable situations, particularly those where concerted information obtaining and high handling needs to take place. A circulated detecting and observing system for the IoT conditions defeat past issues. The point of this proposition is to upgrade the utilization of biomedical sensors and registering assets for having the option to give propelled applications to the client. The structure of a conveyed computational system utilizes the accessible figuring abilities of the brilliant gadgets for sharing the preparation of cutting edge wellbeing observing applications.

Cambra *et al*, (2017) [111] suggests the plan of a keen IoT correspondence framework. It aims to minimize the effort of the water system controller. The proposition is a water system device that collects ongoing information, for example, the variable water system rate. Information handled in a cloud administration is dependent on the Drools Guvnor. The created mixed-media stage controls remotely by a cell phone. The data transmission devoured when the framework is sending various types of directions is estimated.

Kang *et al*, (2015) [112] suggested an IoT-based observing framework utilizing a tri-level setting model. The design is an administration in an intelligent home system. It moreover shows a setting based brilliant home assistance employs a real model and administration situation for future IoT conditions. Each degree of the proposed setting making model has diverse help types. They are a primary checking administration with a programmed controlled and client-driven assistance.

The methodology [113] is dependent on a two-arrange situation for surveying the freshness of in-travel organic products. In the principal organization, the authors have utilized a learning-by-doing component in building up a situation development technique. The system aims to consequently obtain the fittest conveyance condition and the event likelihood for every situation. In the subsequent stage, they have incorporated with the interim correlation strategy into the situation examination technique to address the freshness appraisal of in-travel natural products.

ISSUES AND CHALLENGES

Sensors are tiny devices aiming to provide better benefits to their clients. These unsupervised nodes have their challenges. The summary details this section:

Security

The vast majority of the dangers and assaults exist [114] in remote systems. They are practically wired associates with exacerbation with the consideration of remote availability. The unguided transmission medium is more vulnerable to security assaults than those of the guided transmission medium. The communication idea of remote correspondence is a straightforward contender for listening. In the majority of the cases, different security issues [115] and dangerous identification with those considered for remote appointed systems are pertinent for remote sensor systems. Based on the characteristics, the classification falls. Fig. (2) represents the classification of security attacks in WSN.

TinySec [117] is the first thoroughly executed connection layer security engineering for remote sensor systems. TinySec is convenient for an assortment of equipment and radio stages. The creator structures a lightweight and efficient link-layer security convention. TinySec bolsters two distinctive security alternatives - verified encryption (TinySec-AE) and verification (TinySec-Auth).

Zhan *et al.* (2006) [118] suggest area-based keys by restricting private keys of individual hubs to both their IDs and geographic areas. The creators build up an LBK-based neighborhood validation plan to confine the effect of traded off devices on their region. They presented proficient ways to deal with setting up a mutual key between any two system hubs. The methodology approaches include absolute strength to hub bargain, stunted correspondence and calculation overhead, fewer memory prerequisites, and soaring system versatility.

The system [119] characterizes the sorts of information existing in sensor arranges and recognize agreeable correspondence security dangers as indicated by that order. The creators propose a correspondence security plot where they characterize the particulars to a relating security component. Rules formulation uses this multi-tiered security engineering. Hence, every instrument has distinctive asset necessities.

The recommendation [120] is a novel area-based methodology where the mystery keys are bound to geographic areas. Every hub stores a couple of solution dependent on its location. The area restricting property compels the degree for which individual credentials misuse along these lines constraints the harms brought about by an assortment of traded off hubs. The issue of report creation assaults is used to detail the problem.

The proposed security enhancements [121] fuses with the [122] accomplishing a progressively secure and robust two-calculate client confirmation WSNs. The scheme proves that clients cannot change/update their passwords. It does not give the same validation between entryway hub and sensor hub and is powerless against passage hub bypassing assault and insider assault.

The suggestion [123] is an area-aware strategy security system wherein every hub stores a couple of mystery keys. Those mystery keys are bound to the hub's geographic area. The property of the area-aware keys effectively constrains the effect of traded off devices on their region. The creators propose a multifunctional credential administration structure which guarantees both node-to-sink and hub-to-hub verification along report sending courses. Also, the novel one-to-numerous information conveyance approach ensures efficient on the way of counterfeit information sifting and is exceptionally powerful against DoS assaults.

Park and Shin (2004) [124] suggested a lightweight security protocol (LiSP) that makes a tradeoff among security and asset utilization proficient rekeying. The core of the convention is the novel rekeying system that offers - effective key communication without requiring retransmission/ACKs, verification for each key-divulgence without bringing about extra overhead. It also supports the capacity of identifying/recuperating lost keys and consistent credential refreshment without disturbing continuous information encryption/unscrambling.

Ferreira *et al.* (2005) [125] researches the issue of adding security to cluster-based correspondence conventions for homogeneous remote sensor systems comprising of sensor hubs with constrained assets. They propose a security answer for LEACH is a convention where group shapes are progressive and intermittent. The vitality is an efficient security convention proposal [126] utilizing symmetric cryptographic calculations to help security. To alleviate the downsides of symmetric cryptographic reckon the session key is changed progressively.

The suggested innovation [127] identifies the sensor organize as having a hub design. It aims performance by trusting neighboring sensor hubs and the board of next-door sensor hubs for checking security in the sensor arrange. The sensor organization incorporates a base station and a majority of sensor hubs for detailing detected data bundles to the base station through radiofrequency signals transferred by other sensor hubs. A judge sensor hub may have a trust estimator in its hub engineering to assess the reliability of a neighboring sensor hub by deciding an individual reference and getting the solo reference from jury sensor hubs. Given the dependability of the suspect, the judge may change a course for transmitting bundles to the base station.

Hsiao & Hwan (2010) [128] proposed a productive key administration plot and utilization of symmetric cryptography to verify the messages. The proposed plan further ensures the goal ought to get the information effectively. iDetect [129] is a multi-objective hereditary calculation-based interruption identification framework (IDS). It gives ideal assault recognition in the system. The proposed calculation ensures highlights fundamental for distinguishing particular assault utilization in the interruption discovery process.

The work [130] receives the seed of key mapping innovation. It joins a couple of credential variables into several differing sensor devices and utilizations. Elliptic key cryptography and structures a public key relating to a similar two private keys that are utilized as encryption key and unscrambling key separately. The usage of keys is shared credential data between contiguous hubs. The procedure benefits of security, stockpiling execution, and vitality utilization. The recommendation [131] utilizes character-based encryption to help vitality utilization. The creators have created two varieties of the proposed arrangement relying upon the way and when assault identification happens.

Energy

Energy is a primary resource to keep the devices running. Minimizing energy consumption prolongs the lifespan of the devices.

The creator proposes [132] to incorporate a nearby power Source. The vitality collector may have a related radio reception apparatus that harvests AM radio waves ubiquitously. The radio recurrence frequency energy harvested may be Stored utilizing a Supercapacitor. The put-away vitality may control an independent handling unit straightforwardly when the degree of the vital gathered stays over an edge level.

The system [133] is an ideal group-based instrument by a changed multi-bounce layered model. Its uses include in load offsetting with numerous versatile sinks. Under the state of a postponement, meeting hubs (RNs) usage understands the objective of ideal vitality utilization in the feeling of vitality transmission model through a heuristic calculation in a graphical manner. The system [134] is a meta-heuristic improvement method. Cuckoo Search (CS) computes total information in the Sensor Network. The least vitality hubs mold as subordinate chains (or) groups for detecting the information and high vitality hubs as Cluster Head for conveying to the Base Station (BS). The adjusted CS proposal improves the system execution fusing adjusted vitality dispersal and results in the development of an ideal number of bunches and insignificant vitality utilization.

MCR convention [135] depends on isolating the system into dynamic bunches. The bunch heads decision depends on the weighted likelihood. The group's hubs speak with a chosen bunch head hub by utilizing a single jump correspondence approach. The group heads impart the data to the base station by employing a multi-bounce correspondence approach.

Adaptive Collection Scheme-Based Matrix Completion (ACMC) [136] is a suggestion that is a contrasted and conventional information assortment scheme. The information assortment plans fluctuate with the accessible vitality, gathering a lot of information when the accessible vital is adequate to acquire excellent information-based applications. The ACMC conspire likewise and proposes a technique for diminishing the postponement by expanding the obligation cycle of the hubs that are a long way from the CC.

The recommendation [137] is a Forecasting-based Monitoring and Tomography (FMT) structure is exhibiting for WSNs. The goal of the FMT system is to accomplish to catch the tomography of the accessible vitality in WSNs with the least vitality use. The FMT system joins accessible vital estimating and arranges total components to lessen the measure of vital devoured for checking motivation. Fuzzy Logic Scheme (FLS) [138] applies to the hub's choice. Conversely, with the cases of one descriptor, the FLS application can deal with the deferral/vitality tradeoffs to meet the system execution necessities. The separation of a hub to the source hub chooses as predecessors for the FLS. The yield of FLS gave altering components to the SIR edge.

The proposal is [139] a progressively evenhanded and stochastic procedure which disperses consistently the vitality expended through the entire system to choose the Cluster Head (CH). This convention utilization improves vitality productivity conveyance where the BS is restricted far away from the system. Besides, its employment is where the gathered information characterizes the greatest or the base qualities in the directed locale. Enhanced Low Energy Clustering Protocol (ELECP) [140] is a decentralized bunching calculation used for the situation where the zone detected information is not flawlessly associated. The method segment the system, permitting the dispersion of vitality load among any sensor hubs.

Hardware Related Issues

A remote sensor arrangement is a gathering of profoundly obliged equipment stages considered sensor hubs that team up towards a lot of shared objectives. All the more explicitly, those objectives are observing, cautioning, and provisioning of data to the system. A large portion of the usefulness of a sensor arrangement is information-driven, although it is additionally conceivable to utilize it as a conveyed figuring stage under exclusive conditions. A remote sensor hub has worked in sensors, constrained computational abilities, and communicates through an isolated channel. Devices are small in size, and can inconspicuously give the physical data of any entity. They are battery-fueled that can act freely and work self-directive whenever required.

The inside design [68, 141] of the system is how the hubs bunch themselves to accomplish their objectives. Some of the problems traced are analyzed to give solutions for the same. The section explains various authors' suggestions.

The work [142] is a reciprocal methodology that neglects the equipment outline separating capacities given by radio handsets. The proposal [143] is a methodology designed for checking the pipeline and prescribing support and fixes it in exclusive areas. Upkeep incorporates the discovery of consumption utilizing sensors that can bring about holes.

The recommendation [144] is an improved model with levels for investigating sensors with movable transmission runs in a WSN with the roundabout multijump organization. Based on the model, the correct transmission scopes of sensors in every cluster are the choice factor for upgrading the system lifetime after hubs sending. The work [145] is a power-sharing calculation dependent on the game hypothesis. Its actualization in FPGA for an installed remote framework wherein both Primary User (PU) and cognitive radio sensor nodes (CRSN) work all the while and a devoted equipment unit takes the choice about the power transmission for both PU and CRSN.

Localization

Area-based directing conventions [146] depend on the area data where the sensor devices deployment. The benefits of location routing conventions incorporate better versatility and less overhead brought about by robust changes in topology. It utilizes area data to acquire a lot of littler solicitation zone than the potential looking region for directing ways. The usage of the areas of the device provides references to encourage recognizable proof and correspondence inside a system. The below readings are some of the solutions provided by various authors towards localizing [147] the sensors in the environments.

Semidefinite programming (SDP) unwinding based technique [148] is for the position estimation issue in remote sensor systems. The streamlining concern limits the blunder in sensor positions to fit separation measures. Discernible measures check the nature of the point estimation of sensors or to recognize inappropriate sensors. SDP based model and technique [149] for the position is part of the work. The creators use SDP duality and inside guide calculation speculations toward demonstrating that the SDP limits of any system or a diagram that has exceptional sensor positions to fit given separation measures.

A general SDP based methodology [150] for fathoming the chart acknowledgment issue is the sensor arranges confinement problem. The creators portray two enhancements to enhance such trouble. To start with, they propose a regularization term in the target work that can diminish the position of the SDP arrangement. Second, they use the SDP arrangement as the underlying emphasis for a slope drop strategy. It additionally refines the assessed focuses. A lower bound acquired from the ideal SDP target worth employs to check the arrangement quality.

The Received Signal Strength (RSS) based limitation [151] procedures undergo partitioning into two categories - the separation estimation based and the RSS profiling based systems. The creators [152] propose a few processes for the online alignment of the Path Loss Exponent (PLE) [153] in remote sensor systems without depending on separation estimations. The work [154] applies to finish the missing separations in the portion grid. The yield of the proposed procedure is combined with Helmert's change to refine the last area estimation with the assistance of visits.

Strumberger *et al.*, (2018) [155] is elephant herding optimization calculation (EHO). The proposal takes care of limitation issues in remote sensor systems. EHO is a generally new swarm knowledge metaheuristic that gets promising outcomes when managing NP difficult issues. The work [156] is a stochastic canny improvement technique dependent on the state change calculation with tackling Sensor Network Lifetime (SNL) issue. It performs without additional suspicions and conditions on the problem structure. To rise above nearby optimality, a robust change procedure called "hazard and reclamation in probability" is joined into the state progress calculation. The strained state change calculation applies to the SNL issue, and palatable reenactment results show the viability of the proposed methodology.

The recommendation [157] is a two-phase calculation with a semi-versatile method that utilizes swarm methodology to calculate. The system [158] is a wireless integrated network sensor (WINS) framework. It incorporates frame with WINS arrange as well as visual or infrared sensors and imaging gadgets. It empowers the demand and focuses on tracking through a sensor field or past solitary coordinated detection to focus on the unit. The sensors with signal preparation utilization trigger the cameras and the following frameworks. It gives an elective area capacity to improve strength. The frame is self-arranging and remotely controllable and empowers remote frameworks. Its administrator provisions querying the gathered information - noticeable, picture information, and controls of the structure.

Saeed *et al*, (2018) [154] figures the issue of missing pairwise separations and exceptions as an advancement issue. It comprehends through half quadratic minimization. The work [159] is a technique for improving a customary without range based limitation strategy. It utilizes delicate registering approaches in a hybrid model. This model coordinates a rationale framework. The utilizations of the learning machine (ELM) enhancement procedure to gain by the qualities of the two methodologies have provided improvement in the structure. The proportions of known devices inside the detecting inclusion range are known as hubs.The detecting inclusion range to the highest inclusion run as versatile loads for this crossbreed model. The idea of resultant power vectors application to the hybrid model over swarm streamlining relieves the impacts of unpredictable arrangements.

A framework [160] includes various gadgets such that each has a sensor arrangement speaks with different devices suggested. The frame further incorporates a controller arranged to give direction to data that indicates a method of activity of the gadgets. In the first method, the instrument transmits correspondence signals. The invigorated device adjusts to correspondence signals from underlying quality dependent on correspondence signals it gets from at least one different gadget. In the second method, the gadgets transmit correspondence signals. The invigorated device progressively modifies the correspondence signal based correspondence signals it gets from at least one different device and on estimations performed by the sensor in the given instrument. The work [161] is a sensor hub having a self-confinement and a self-limitation strategy for the sensor hub. The sensor hub ascertains an area. Estimation is made from one of two portable devices on various occasions and utilizing received data. The extra cost and power utilization required for introducing additional hardware are a sign enhancer is decreased.

Understanding the pros and cons of the system a list rendering the same made and represented in the table. The SWOT analysis provides a list of strengths, weaknesses, opportunities, and threats to the system. Table **1** provides the SWOT analysis of WSN.

Table 1. Strength, Weakness, Opportunities and Threat (SWOT) analysis of WSN [162].

Strength	Weakness	Opportunities	Threat
Suitable for any adverse and unCondusive Ambience	Process might be slow compare to wired network	Innovation	Insecure network
Economically Feasible	Process might be hinder by surroundings	Technological advancement	Regulatory issues by statutory governing bodies
Time is not a constrain for incorporation of new device	Distractions might happen due to usage of Bluetooth	New business field for the tycoons	Non-Awareness
Control system can be managed by central system	Limited Battery power and storage		

OVERVIEW OF THE BOOK

The book details the usage of sensors in various applications, the significance of sensors in building IoT devices, the support provided by cloud and fog computation to store sensed information on their servers.

The sensors are tiny devices used to detect the environment or track any object of interest. They are self-configuring devices that aid in minimizing human efforts. The book details the usage of sensors in various applications, the significance of sensors in building IoT devices, the support provided by cloud and fog computation to store sensed information on their servers.

Though sensors have made a lot of difference in human life, they show some shortcomings. IoT tries to find some answers to these drawbacks. Intelligent sensors working as IoT segments convert this present reality variable that they are estimating into a digital information stream for transmission to a gateway. Internet of Things (IoT) applications, regardless of whether for city foundations, plants, or wearable devices, utilize enormous varieties of sensors gathering information for transmission over the Internet to a focal, cloud-based figuring asset. The second chapter describes contributions made towards the architecture and working of IoT, its usage, and use cases challenge the technology is facing, and future directions for further research. The section details Five-layered and other architectures. The division narrates IoT objects and data. The part also describes various use cases - hut architecture, FIT IoT-LAB testbed, and others. An elaboration made includes Object identification, authentication, and authorization.

The sensor system may comprise of various sensor hubs following up together to screen a district and get information about the environment. As of now, WSNs usage in a few regions like medicinal services, barriers, for example, military objective following and observation, government and ecological administrations like cataclysmic event alleviation, perilous condition investigation, and seismic detecting, *etc*. For checking the enormous condition, there is a restricted correspondence between hubs because of obstacles into nature, which thus influences the typical system topology. Sensors are low in storage. Cloud with IoT is aiming to backup the information gathered by these devices. Investigation programming running on the cloud PCs lessens the enormous volumes of created information into notable data for clients and directions to actuators retreat in the field. The third chapter talks about the contributions made towards the different cloud computing arena. Its architecture suggestions by various authors summarize this chapter. The limitations, challenges, the use of the technology in many applications with use case discussions make this chapter. The division details the features containing scalability & flexibility, autonomous systems, on-demand service provisioning, and user-centric interfaces. The applications mentioned in use cases talk about the usage of cloud technology in the sensor/IoT domain. Elaboration of applications comprised of agriculture, healthcare, solar energy, smart city, homes, and industry. The section also details advantages containing elasticity, virtualization, enormous scale figuring systems, gathering aggregate knowledge, information streaming, and sensor interfacing with cloud, complicated occasion preparation, Monstrous scaling & constant preparation. Some of the challenges are under consideration. It details interoperability, heterogeneity, security, and privacy.

Portability adds wings to the technology. It provides flexibility to its users. Mobile Cloud computing (MCC) is available in either cell phone or any other hand versatile implanted framework. Portable processing is coordinating with distributed computing on account of the fundamental attributes of the cloud model. The fourth chapter provides a vision into the taxonomy of the system, its security issues, management issues, advantages, applications, challenges, and future directions. Computation offloading, multi-tier programming, live-cloud streaming, and remote data managing are the taxonomy issues detailed. The pros, applications discussed are sensor/IoT focused. The division contains the description of storage, flexibility, cost efficiency, mobility & availability, backup & disaster recovery, resiliency & redundancy, scalability & performance, quick deployment & ease integration, environment friendly. The chapter includes challenges like heterogeneity, quality of service, and security & privacy.

Edge devices do not provide a smooth flow of information. Fog computation usage provides efficient communication in these devices. Fog processing is a dispersed figuring worldview that goes about in the middle of Cloud datacenters and IoT gadgets/sensors. It offers calculations, systems administration, and storerooms. Hence, Cloud-based administrations stretch out nearer to the IoT gadgets/sensors. Cloud data centers are geologically intensive. They frequently neglect to manage capacity and preparing requests of billions of geo-dispersed IoT gadgets/sensors. Accordingly, the clogged system, high inactivity in administration conveyance, low quality of Service (QoS) experience are the disadvantages. The fifth chapter talks about the taxonomy, challenges, and future directions towards Fog computation. The division details taxonomy compromises fog node configuration, nodal collaboration, resource/service provisioning metrics, service level objectives, applicable network system, and security concern.

The Internet of Things (IoT) worldview depends on astute and self-designing hubs interconnected in a dynamic and worldwide system foundation. IoT portrays by authentic little things, generally conveyed, with restricted stockpiling and handling limits, which include concerns concerning unwavering quality, execution, security, and protection. Cloud registering has boundless abilities as far as capacity and preparing power, is a substantially more experienced innovation, and has the majority of the IoT issues at any rate mostly unraveled. A novel IT worldview in which Cloud and IoT are two reciprocal advances consolidated are relied upon to build the future. This sixth chapter summarizes the integrated system, its applications, use cases, and some of the open issues. It details scalability and storage characteristics. The system utilizes the IoT Device Delegate to control every gadget from numerous clouds and Intention Manager to oversee the connection between gadgets. The applications will be able to transmit data to the cloud without using versatile terminals. It aims to create a smart and flexible environment. It elaborates applications comprising of healthcare and an intelligent environment. It also details use cases like Cloud4IoT, TOSCA, *etc*. It explains challenges like security and availability.

REFERENCES

[1]   I.F. Akyildiz, W. Su, Y. Sankarasubramaniam, and E. Cayirci, "A survey on sensor networks", *IEEE Commun. Mag.,* vol. 40, no. 8, pp. 102-114, 2002.
[http://dx.doi.org/10.1109/MCOM.2002.1024422]

[2]   Y.Y. Sergey, and M.T.S. Gomes, *Smart Sensors and MEMS,* S Nihtianov, A. Luque, Eds., 2nded. Sensors.: swaston, UK, 2005.

[3]   J. Deng, R. Hang, and S. Mishra, "Limiting Dos attacks during multihop data delivery in wireless sensor network", *Int. J. Secur. Net.,* vol. 1, no. 3-4, pp. 167-178.
[http://dx.doi.org/10.1504/IJSN.2006.011776]

[4]   F. Yulin, and S. Xiangning, "Improvement on LEACH protocol of wireless sensor network", In: *International Conference on Sensor Technologies and Applications.* Valencia, Spain, 2007, pp. 260-264.

[5]   J. A. Stankovic, "Wireless sensor networks for in-home healthcare: Potential and challenges", In: *High confidence medical device software and systems (HCMDSS) workshop.* Philadelphia, PA, 2005, pp. 1-4.

[6]   T. Arampatzis, J. Lygeros, and S. Manesis, "A survey of applications of wireless sensors and wireless sensor networks", *Mediterrean Conference on Control and Automation Intelligent Control,* 2005, pp. 719-724 Limassol, Cyprus.
[http://dx.doi.org/10.1109/.2005.1467103]

[7]   S.H. Lee, S. Lee, H. Song, and H.S. Lee, "Wireless sensor network design for tactical military applications: Remote large-scale environments", In: *IEEE Military communications conference.* MILCOM: Boston, MA, USA, 2009, pp. 1-7.

[8]   Mainwaring, "Wireless sensor networks for habitat monitoring", In: *1ˢᵗ ACM international workshop on Wireless sensor networks and applications.* Atlanta, Georgia, USA, 2002, pp. 88-97.
[http://dx.doi.org/10.1145/570738.570751]

[9]   B. Rashid, and M.H. Rehmani, "Applications of wireless sensor networks for urban areas: A survey", *J. Netw. Comput. Appl.,* vol. 60, pp. 192-219, 2016.
[http://dx.doi.org/10.1016/j.jnca.2015.09.008]

[10]   A. Agah, S.K. Das, K. Basu, and M. Asadi, "Intrusion detection in sensor networks: A non-cooperative game approach", *Third IEEE International Symposium on Network Computing and Applications,* 2004, pp. 343-346 Cambridge, MA, USA.

[11]   I. Krontiris, T. Dimitriou, T. Giannetsos, and M. Mpasoukos, "Intrusion detection of sinkhole attacks in wireless sensor networks", *International symposium on algorithms and experiments for sensor systems, wireless networks and distributed robotics,* 2007, pp. 150-161 Reykjavik, Iceland.

[12]   K.C. Lee, W.C. Lee, B. Zheng, and J. Winter, "Processing multiple aggregation queries in geo-sensor networks", *International Conference on Database Systems for Advanced Applications,* 2006, pp. 20-34 New Delhi, India.
[http://dx.doi.org/10.1007/11733836_4]

[13]   S.C.H. Huang, M.X. Cheng, and D.Z. Du, "GeoSENS: geo-based sensor network secure communication protocol", *Comput. Commun.,* vol. 29, no. 4, pp. 456-461, 2006.
[http://dx.doi.org/10.1016/j.comcom.2004.12.030]

[14]   M.L. McKelvin Jr, M.L. Williams, and N.M. Berry, "Integrated radio frequency identification and wireless sensor network architecture for automated inventory management and tracking applications", *Proceedings of the 2005 Conference on Diversity in Computing,* 2005, pp. 44-47 Albuquerque New Mexico USA.

[15]   T. Chen, "System and apparatus of Internet-linked RFID sensor network for object identifying, sensing, monitoring, tracking and networking", *Software,* vol. 11/141, p. 762, 2006.

[16]   C. Brignone, T. Connors, G. Lyon, and S. Pradhan, "SmartLOCUS: An autonomous, self-assembling sensor network for indoor asset and systems management", *Mobile Media Syst. Lab., HP Laboratories, Palo Alto, CA, Tech. Rep,* p. 41.

[17]   Z. Sun, "MISE-PIPE: Magnetic induction-based wireless sensor networks for underground pipeline monitoring", *Ad Hoc Netw.,* vol. 9, no. 3, pp. 218-227, 2011.
[http://dx.doi.org/10.1016/j.adhoc.2010.10.006]

[18]   I. Stoianov, L. Nachman, S. Madden, and T. Tokmouline, "PIPENETa wireless sensor network for pipeline monitoring", *Proceedings of the 6ᵗʰ international conference on Information processing in sensor networks,* 2007, pp. 264-273 Cambridge, Massachusetts, USA.
[http://dx.doi.org/10.1145/1236360.1236396]

[19]   J.G. Rodrigues, A. Aguiar, and J. Barros, "Sensemycity: Crowdsourcing an urban sensor", *Comput. Soc.,* pp. 1-10, 2014.

[20]   T. Heinemann, A. Latanzio, and F. Roveda, "The Eumetsat multi-sensor precipitation estimate (MPE", *Second International Precipitation Working group (IPWG) Meeting,* 2002, pp. 23-27 Colorado.

[21]   G. Yang, *Body sensor networks.,* G.Z. Yang, Ed., vol. 1. 1ˢᵗ ed. Springer: London, UK, 2006.
[http://dx.doi.org/10.1007/1-84628-484-8]

[22]   G. Fortino, R. Giannantonio, R. Gravina, P. Kuryloski, and R. Jafari, "Enabling effective programming and flexible management of efficient body sensor network applications", *IEEE Trans. Hum. Mach. Syst.,* vol. 43, no. 1, pp. 115-133, 2012.
[http://dx.doi.org/10.1109/TSMCC.2012.2215852]

[23]   M. Li, W. Lou, and K. Ren, "Data security and privacy in wireless body area networks", *IEEE Wirel. Commun.,* vol. 17, no. 1, pp. 51-58, 2010.
[http://dx.doi.org/10.1109/MWC.2010.5416350]

[24]   B.P. Lo, S. Thiemjarus, R. King, and G.Z. Yang, "Body sensor network-a wireless sensor platform for pervasive healthcare monitoring", *3ʳᵈ International conference on Pervasive Computing,* 2005, pp. 77-80 Munich, Germany.

[25]   A. Darwish, and A.E. Hassanien, "Wearable and implantable wireless sensor network solutions for healthcare monitoring", *Sensors (Basel),* vol. 11, no. 6, pp. 5561-5595, 2011.
[http://dx.doi.org/10.3390/s110605561] [PMID: 22163914]

[26]   B.H. Yang, and S. Rhee, "Development of the ring sensor for healthcare automation", *Robot. Auton. Syst.,* vol. 30, no. 3, pp. 273-281, 2000.
[http://dx.doi.org/10.1016/S0921-8890(99)00092-5]

[27]   T.Q. Trung, and N.E. Lee, "Flexible and stretchable physical sensor integrated platforms for wearable human-activity monitoring and personal healthcare", *Adv. Mater.,* vol. 28, no. 22, pp. 4338-4372, 2016.
[http://dx.doi.org/10.1002/adma.201504244] [PMID: 26840387]

[28]   J.M. Corchado, J. Bajo, D.I. Tapia, and A. Abraham, "Using heterogeneous wireless sensor networks in a telemonitoring system for healthcare", *IEEE Trans. Inf. Technol. Biomed.,* vol. 14, no. 2, pp. 234-240, 2010.
[http://dx.doi.org/10.1109/TITB.2009.2034369] [PMID: 19858034]

[29]   Yanchuan Cao Shanshan, and Sameer Iyengar Jiang, "CareNet: an integrated wireless sensor networking environment for remote healthcare,", *BODYNETS,* p. 9, 2008.

[30]   V. Boonsawat, J. Ekchamanonta, K. Bumrungkhet, and S. Kittipiyakul, "XBee wireless sensor networks for temperature monitoring", In: *Second conference on application research and development (ECTI-CARD 2010),* Chon Buri, Thailand, 2010, pp. 221-226.

[31]   A. Vaz, "Full passive UHF tag with a temperature sensor suitable for human body temperature monitoring", *IEEE Trans. Circuits Syst., II Express Briefs,* vol. 57, no. 2, pp. 95-99, 2010.
[http://dx.doi.org/10.1109/TCSII.2010.2040314]

[32]   V. Jelicic, M. Magno, D. Brunelli, G. Paci, and L. Benini, "Context-adaptive multimodal wireless sensor network for energy-efficient gas monitoring", *IEEE Sens. J.,* vol. 13, no. 1, pp. 328-338, 2012.
[http://dx.doi.org/10.1109/JSEN.2012.2215733]

[33]   A. Somov, "Development of wireless sensor network for combustible gas monitoring", *Sens. Actuators A Phys.,* vol. 171, no. 2, pp. 398-405, 2011.

[http://dx.doi.org/10.1016/j.sna.2011.07.016]

[34] J. A. Gu, C. Y. Wu, M. K. Donnelly, and J. C. Kwok, "Electrical power system sensor devices, electrical power system monitoring methods, and electrical power system monitoring systems", *Software 8,560,256,* 2013. October 15.

[35] M. Hempstead, N. Tripathi, P. Mauro, G.Y. Wei, and D. Brooks, "An ultra low power system architecture for sensor network applications", *32nd International Symposium on Computer Architecture (ISCA '05),* 2005, pp. 208-219 Madison, WI, USA.
[http://dx.doi.org/10.1109/ISCA.2005.12]

[36] R.H. Bhuiyan, R.A. Dougal, and M. Ali, "A miniature energy harvesting device for wireless sensors in electric power system", *IEEE Sens. J.,* vol. 10, no. 7, pp. 1249-1258, 2010.
[http://dx.doi.org/10.1109/JSEN.2010.2040173]

[37] B. Maag, Z. Zhou, and L. Thiele, "A survey on sensor calibration in air pollution monitoring deployments", *IEEE Inter. Things J.,* vol. 5, no. 6, pp. 4857-4870, 2018.
[http://dx.doi.org/10.1109/JIOT.2018.2853660]

[38] K.K. Khedo, R. Perseedoss, and A. Mungur, "A wireless sensor network air pollution monitoring system", *Int. J. Wire. Mob. Net.,* vol. 2, no. 2, pp. 31-45, 2010.
[http://dx.doi.org/10.5121/ijwmn.2010.2203]

[39] A.R. Al-Ali, "Imran Zualkernan, and Fadi Aloul, "A mobile GPRS-sensors array for air pollution monitoring", *IEEE Sens. J.,* vol. 10, no. 10, pp. 1666-1672, 2010.
[http://dx.doi.org/10.1109/JSEN.2010.2045890]

[40] F. Bovolo, and L. Bruzzone, "A split-based approach to unsupervised change detection in large-size multitemporal images: Application to tsunami-damage assessment", *IEEE Trans. Geosci. Remote Sens.,* vol. 45, no. 6, pp. 1658-1670, 2007.
[http://dx.doi.org/10.1109/TGRS.2007.895835]

[41] Anna Dzvonkovskaya, and Klaus-Werner Gurgel, "Future Contribution of HF Radar WERA to Tsunami Early Warning Systems", *Eur. J. Navig.,* vol. 7, no. 2, pp. 1-7, 2009.

[42] H.R. Bogena, J.A. Huisman, C. Oberdörster, and H. Vereecken, "Evaluation of a low-cost soil water content sensor for wireless network applications", *J. Hydrol. (Amst.),* vol. 344, no. 1-2, pp. 32-42, 2007.
[http://dx.doi.org/10.1016/j.jhydrol.2007.06.032]

[43] R. Cardell-Oliver, M. Kranz, K. Smettem, and K. Mayer, "A reactive soil moisture sensor network: Design and field evaluation", *Int. J. Distrib. Sens. Netw.,* vol. 1, no. 2, pp. 149-162, 2005.
[http://dx.doi.org/10.1080/15501320590966422]

[44] H.R. Bogena, "Potential of wireless sensor networks for measuring soil water content variability", *Vadose Zone J.,* vol. 9, no. 4, pp. 1002-1013, 2010.
[http://dx.doi.org/10.2136/vzj2009.0173]

[45] J. Gutiérrez, J.F. Villa-Medina, A. Nieto-Garibay, and M.Á. Porta-Gándara, "Automated Irrigation System Using a Wireless Sensor Network and GPRS Module", *IEEE Trans. Instrum. Meas.,* vol. 63, no. 1, pp. 166-176, 2014.
[http://dx.doi.org/10.1109/TIM.2013.2276487]

[46] H. Peijina, J. Tingb, and Z. Yandongc, "Monitoring system of soil water content based on zigbee wireless sensor network", *Nongye Gongcheng Xuebao (Beijing),* vol. 4, 2011.

[47] C. Ayday, and S. Safak, "Application of wireless sensor networks with GIS on the soil moisture distribution mapping", *Symposium GIS,* 2009, pp. 1-6 Ostrava.

[48] Y. Kim, R.G. Evans, and W.M. Iversen, "Evaluation of closed-loop site-specific irrigation with wireless sensor network", *J. Irrig. Drain. Eng.,* vol. 135, no. 1, pp. 25-31, 2009.
[http://dx.doi.org/10.1061/(ASCE)0733-9437(2009)135:1(25)]

[49] R. Morais, A. Valente, and C. Serôdio, "A wireless sensor network for smart irrigation and environmental monitoring: A position article.," In: *5th European federation for information technology in agriculture, food and environment and 3rd world congress on computers in agriculture and natural resources*, Vilareal, Portugal, 2005, pp. 845-850.

[50] D.C. Hymer, M.S. Moran, and T.O. Keefer, "Soil water evaluation using a hydrologic model and calibrated sensor network", *Soil Sci. Soc. Am. J.,* vol. 64, no. 1, pp. 319-326, 2000.
[http://dx.doi.org/10.2136/sssaj2000.641319x]

[51] L. Hui, W. Mao-hua, W. Yue-xuan, M. Dao-kun, and L. Hai-xia, "Development of farmland soil moisture and temperature monitoring system based on wireless sensor network", *J. Jilin Uni.,* vol. 3, pp. 604-608, 2008.

[52] E.P. Stuntebeck, D. Pompili, and T. Melodia, "Wireless underground sensor networks using commodity terrestrial motes", *2nd IEEE Workshop on Wireless Mesh Networks,* 2006, pp. 112-114 Reston, VA, USA.
[http://dx.doi.org/10.1109/WIMESH.2006.288625]

[53] R. Szewczyk, "Habitat monitoring with sensor networks", *Center for Embedded Network Sensing,* vol. 47, no. 6, pp. 33-40, 2004.

[54] H. Wang, D. Estrin, and L. Girod, "Preprocessing in a tiered sensor network for habitat monitoring", In: *EURASIP Journal on Applied Signal Processing.* vol. 795089. Marcj, 2003, pp. 392-401.

[55] T. Naumowicz, "Wireless sensor network for habitat monitoring on Skomer Island", *IEEE Local Computer Network Conference,* 2010, pp. 882-889 Denver, CO, USA.
[http://dx.doi.org/10.1109/LCN.2010.5735827]

[56] B. Stojkoska, and D. Davcev, "Web interface for habitat monitoring using wireless sensor network", *Fifth International Conference on Wireless and Mobile Communications,* 2009, pp. 157-162 Cannes, France.
[http://dx.doi.org/10.1109/ICWMC.2009.33]

[57] M. Welsh, D. Malan, B. Duncan, T. Fulford-Jones, and S. Moulton, "Wireless sensor networks for emergency medical care", *GE Global Research Conference,* 2004, p. 1 Boston.

[58] D. S. Lee, Y. D. Lee, W. Y. Chung, and R. Myllyla, "Vital sign monitoring system with life emergency event detection using wireless sensor network", *in SENSORS 2006, Daegu, South Korea,* pp. 518-521, 2006.

[59] S. Li, A. Zhan, X. Wu, P. Yang, and G. Chen, "Efficient Emergency Rescue Navigation with Wireless Sensor Networks", *J. Inf. Sci. Eng.,* vol. 27, no. 1, pp. 51-64, 2011.

[60] X. Liu, G. Li, S. Zhang, and A. Liu, "Big program code dissemination scheme for emergency software-define wireless sensor networks", *Peer-to-Peer Netw. Appl.,* vol. 11, no. 5, pp. 1038-1059, 2018.
[http://dx.doi.org/10.1007/s12083-017-0565-5]

[61] C. Wang, H. Lin, and H. Jiang, "CANS: Towards congestion-adaptive and small stretch emergency navigation with wireless sensor networks", *IEEE Trans. Mobile Comput.,* vol. 15, no. 5, pp. 1077-1089, 2015.
[http://dx.doi.org/10.1109/TMC.2015.2451639]

[62] G. Werner-Allen, "Deploying a wireless sensor network on an active volcano", *IEEE Internet Comput.,* vol. 10, no. 2, pp. 18-25, 2006.
[http://dx.doi.org/10.1109/MIC.2006.26]

[63] Y.C. Tseng, M.S. Pan, and Y.Y. Tsai, "A distributed emergency navigation algorithm for wireless sensor networks", *IEEE Computers,* vol. 39, no. 7, pp. 55-62, 2006.
[http://dx.doi.org/10.1109/MC.2006.248]

[64] T. Gao, "Wireless medical sensor networks in emergency response: Implementation and pilot results",

IEEE Conference on Technologies for Homeland Security, 2008, pp. 187-192 Waltham, MA, USA.
[http://dx.doi.org/10.1109/THS.2008.4534447]

[65]   D. Malan, T. Fulford-Jones, M. Welsh, and S. Moulton, "Codeblue: An ad hoc sensor network infrastructure for emergency medical care", *International workshop on wearable and implantable body sensor networks,* vol. 5, 2004 Germany.

[66]   M. Barnes, H. Leather, and D.K. Arvind, "Emergency evacuation using wireless sensor networks", *32nd IEEE Conference on Local Computer Networks,* 2007, pp. 851-857 Dublin, Ireland.

[67]   Y.C. Tseng, M.S. Pan, and Y.Y. Tsai, "Wireless sensor networks for emergency navigation", *Computer,* vol. 39, no. 7, pp. 55-62, 2006.
[http://dx.doi.org/10.1109/MC.2006.248]

[68]   L. Sitanayah, C.J. Sreenan, and K.N. Brown, "ER-MAC: A hybrid MAC protocol for emergency response wireless sensor networks", *Fourth International Conference on Sensor Technologies and Applications,* 2010, pp. 244-249 Venice, Italy.
[http://dx.doi.org/10.1109/SENSORCOMM.2010.45]

[69]   T. Tabirca, K.N. Brown, and C.J. Sreenan, "A dynamic model for fire emergency evacuation based on wireless sensor networks", *2009 Eighth International Symposium on Parallel and Distributed Computing,* 2009, pp. 29-36 Lisbon, Portugal.
[http://dx.doi.org/10.1109/ISPDC.2009.33]

[70]   Y. Zeng, N. Xiong, J.H. Park, and G. Zheng, "An emergency-adaptive routing scheme for wireless sensor networks for building fire hazard monitoring", *Sensors (Basel),* vol. 10, no. 6, pp. 6128-6148, 2010.
[http://dx.doi.org/10.3390/s100606128] [PMID: 22219706]

[71]   Y.D. Kim, Y.M. Yang, W.S. Kang, and D.K. Kim, "On the design of beacon based wireless sensor network for agricultural emergency monitoring systems", *Comput. Stand. Interfaces,* vol. 36, no. 2, pp. 288-299, 2014.
[http://dx.doi.org/10.1016/j.csi.2011.05.004]

[72]   A. Boukerche, R.B. Araujo, and L. Villas, "A wireless actor and sensor networks QoS-aware routing protocol for the emergency preparedness class of applications", *31st IEEE Conference on Local Computer Networks,* 2006, pp. 832-839 Tampa, FL, USA.
[http://dx.doi.org/10.1109/LCN.2006.322184]

[73]   A. Goel, S. Ray, and N. Chandra, "Intelligent traffic light system to prioritized emergency purpose vehicles based on wireless sensor network", *Int. J. Comput. Appl.,* vol. 40, no. 12, pp. 36-39, 2012.

[74]   C. Setchell, and E.L. Dagless, "Vision-based road-traffic monitoring sensor", *IEE Proc. Vis. Image Signal Process.,* vol. 148, no. 1, pp. 78-84, 2001.
[http://dx.doi.org/10.1049/ip-vis:20010077]

[75]   A. Skordylis, A. Guitton, and N. Trigoni, "Correlation-based data dissemination in traffic monitoring sensor networks", In: *ACM CoNEXT conference* Lisboa, Portugal, 2006, pp. 1-2.
[http://dx.doi.org/10.1145/1368436.1368487]

[76]   X. Li, "Performance evaluation of vehicle-based mobile sensor networks for traffic monitoring", *IEEE Trans. Vehicular Technol.,* vol. 58, no. 4, pp. 1647-1653, 2008.

[77]   D. Butler, and S.H.P.G. Karunaratne, "The suspended solids trap efficiency of the roadside gully pot", *Water Res.,* vol. 29, no. 2, pp. 719-729, 1995.
[http://dx.doi.org/10.1016/0043-1354(94)00149-2]

[78]   C.H. See, K.V. Horoshenkov, R.A. Abd-Alhameed, Y.F. Hu, and S.J. Tait, "A low power wireless sensor network for gully pot monitoring in urban catchments", *IEEE Sens. J.,* vol. 12, no. 5, pp. 1545-1553, 2011.

[79]   J.G. Langeveld, C. de Haan, M. Klootwijk, and R.P.S. Schilperoort, "Monitoring the performance of a storm water separating manifold with distributed temperature sensing", *Water Sci. Technol.,* vol. 66,

no. 1, pp. 145-150, 2012.
[http://dx.doi.org/10.2166/wst.2012.152] [PMID: 22678211]

[80]   A. Dhamdhere, H. Chen, A. Kurusingal, V. Sivaraman, and A. Burdett, "Experiments with wireless sensor networks for real-time athlete monitoring", *IEEE Local Computer Network Conference,* 2010, pp. 938-945 Denver, CO, USA.
[http://dx.doi.org/10.1109/LCN.2010.5735838]

[81]   V. Sivaraman, A. Dhamdhere, H. Chen, A. Kurusingal, and S. Grover, "An experimental study of wireless connectivity and routing in ad hoc sensor networks for real-time soccer player monitoring", *Ad Hoc Netw.,* vol. 11, no. 3, pp. 798-817, 2013.
[http://dx.doi.org/10.1016/j.adhoc.2012.09.005]

[82]   I.F. Akyildiz, and E.P. Stuntebeck, "Wireless underground sensor networks: Research challenges", *Ad Hoc Netw.,* vol. 4, no. 6, pp. 669-686, 2006.
[http://dx.doi.org/10.1016/j.adhoc.2006.04.003]

[83]   M. Li, and Y. Liu, "Underground structure monitoring with wireless sensor networks", *6th International Symposium on Information Processing in Sensor Networks,* 2007, pp. 69-78 Cambridge, Massachusetts, USA.
[http://dx.doi.org/10.1109/IPSN.2007.4379666]

[84]   IV Kail, and A Karl, "Reprogrammable remote sensor monitoring system", *Software 5,959,529, 28 September,* 1999.

[85]   S. H. Shah, and I. Yaqoob, "A survey: Internet of Things (IOT) technologies, applications and challenges", *in IEEE Smart Energy Grid Engineering (SEGE), Oshawa, ON, Canada, August,* pp. 381-385, 2016.
[http://dx.doi.org/10.1109/SEGE.2016.7589556]

[86]   M. T. Lazarescu, "Design of a WSN platform for long-term environmental monitoring for IoT applications", *IEEE J. Emerg. Sel. Top. Cir. Sys.,* vol. 3, no. 1, pp. 45-54, 2013.
[http://dx.doi.org/10.1109/JETCAS.2013.2243032]

[87]   D. Ugrenovic, and G. Gardasevic, "CoAP protocol for Web-based monitoring in IoT healthcare applications," In: *23rd Telecommunications Forum Telfor (TELFOR),* Belgrade, Serbia, 2015, pp. 79-82.
[http://dx.doi.org/10.1109/TELFOR.2015.7377418]

[88]   S.D.T. Kelly, N.K. Suryadevara, and S.C. Mukhopadhyay, "Towards the implementation of IoT for environmental condition monitoring in homes", *IEEE Sens. J.,* vol. 13, no. 10, pp. 3846-3853, 2013.
[http://dx.doi.org/10.1109/JSEN.2013.2263379]

[89]   V.M. Rohokale, N.R. Prasad, and R. Prasad, "A cooperative Internet of Things (IoT) for rural healthcare monitoring and control,"In: *2nd International Conference on Wireless Communication, Vehicular Technology, Information Theory and Aerospace & Electronic Systems Technology (Wireless VITAE),* Chennai, India, 2011, pp. 1-6.
[http://dx.doi.org/10.1109/WIRELESSVITAE.2011.5940920]

[90]   M. Hassanalieragh, "Health monitoring and management using Internet-of-Things (IoT) sensing with cloud-based processing: Opportunities and challenges", *IEEE International Conference on Services Computing,* 2015, pp. 285-292 New York, NY, USA.
[http://dx.doi.org/10.1109/SCC.2015.47]

[91]   L.I.U. Dan, C. Xin, H. Chongwei, and J. Liangliang, "Intelligent agriculture greenhouse environment monitoring system based on IOT technology", *International Conference on Intelligent Transportation, Big Data and Smart City,* 2015, pp. 487-490 Halong Bay, Vietnam.
[http://dx.doi.org/10.1109/ICITBS.2015.126]

[92]   P. Kinney, "Zigbee technology: Wireless control that simply works", In: *Communications design conference.* vol. 2. , 2003, pp. 1-7.

[93] Z. Yang, Q. Zhou, L. Lei, K. Zheng, and W. Xiang, "An IoT-cloud based wearable ECG monitoring system for smart healthcare", *J. Med. Syst.*, vol. 40, no. 12, p. 286, 2016.
[http://dx.doi.org/10.1007/s10916-016-0644-9] [PMID: 27796840]

[94] N. Omidifar, N. Yamani, and A. Yousefi, "The Effect of ECG Training Workshop on Medical Students' Knowledge of ECG Reading and Interpretation, "*Strides in Development of Medical Education*, vol. 3, no. 2, pp. 118-125, 2007.

[95] L. Montulli, "Persistent client state in a hypertext transfer protocol based client-server system", *Software 5,774,670. June 30*, 1998.

[96] S.A. Shinde, P.A. Nimkar, S.P. Singh, V.D. Salpe, and Y.R. Jadhav, "MQTT-message queuing telemetry transport protocol", *Int. J. Res.*, vol. 3, no. 3, pp. 240-244, 2016.

[97] C. Xiaojun, L. Xianpeng, and X. Peng, "IOT-based air pollution monitoring and forecasting system", *International Conference on Computer and Computational Sciences (ICCCS)*, 2015, pp. 257-260 Noida, India.
[http://dx.doi.org/10.1109/ICCACS.2015.7361361]

[98] S. Adhya, D. Saha, A. Das, J. Jana, and H. Saha, "An IoT based smart solar photovoltaic remote monitoring and control unit, "In: *2nd international conference on control, instrumentation, energy & communication (CIEC)*, Kolkata, India, 2016, pp. 432-436.
[http://dx.doi.org/10.1109/CIEC.2016.7513793]

[99] I. Mohanraj, K. Ashokumar, and J. Naren, "Field monitoring and automation using IOT in agriculture domain", *6th International Conference on Advances in Computing and Communications,* vol. 93, 2016, pp. 931-939 Kochi.
[http://dx.doi.org/10.1016/j.procs.2016.07.275]

[100] T. Baranwal, and P.K. Pateriya, *"Development of IoT based smart security and monitoring devices for agriculture.,"* in *6th International Conference-Cloud System and Big Data Engineering.* Confluence: Noida, India, 2016, pp. 597-602.

[101] P. Rajalakshmi, and S.D. Mahalakshmi, "IOT based crop-field monitoring and irrigation automation", *10th International Conference on Intelligent Systems and Control (ISCO)*, 2016, pp. 1-6 Coimbatore, India.
[http://dx.doi.org/10.1109/ISCO.2016.7726900]

[102] N. Suma, S. R. Samson, S. Saranya, G. Shanmugapriya, and R. Subhashri, "IOT based smart agriculture monitoring system", *Int. J. Rec. Innov. Tre. Com. Communi.*, vol. 5, no. 2, pp. 177-181, February 2017.

[103] G. Mois, S. Folea, and T. Sanislav, "Analysis of three IoT-based wireless sensors for environmental monitoring", *IEEE Trans. Instrum. Meas.*, vol. 66, no. 8, pp. 2056-2064, 2017.
[http://dx.doi.org/10.1109/TIM.2017.2677619]

[104] C. Partridge, and S. Pink, "A faster UDP (user datagram protocol)", *IEEE/ACM Trans. Netw.*, vol. 1, no. 4, pp. 429-440, 1993.
[http://dx.doi.org/10.1109/90.251895]

[105] Y.C. Cheng, Y. Chawathe, A. LaMarca, and J. Krumm, "Accuracy characterization for metropolitan-scale Wi-Fi localization,"In: *3rd international conference on Mobile systems, applications, and services*, Seattle, Washington , 2005, pp. 233-245.
[http://dx.doi.org/10.1145/1067170.1067195]

[106] S. Manna, S.S. Bhunia, and N. Mukherjee, "Vehicular pollution monitoring using IoT", *International Conference on Recent Advances and Innovations in Engineering (ICRAIE-2014)*, 2014, pp. 1-5 Jaipur, India.

[107] S.V. Zanjal, and G.R. Talmale, "Medicine reminder and monitoring system for secure health using IOT", In: *International Conference on Information Security & Privacy (ICISP2015)*, Nagpur, INDIA, 2016, pp. 471-476.

[http://dx.doi.org/10.1016/j.procs.2016.02.090]

[108] N. Sinha, K.E. Pujitha, and J.S.R. Alex, "Xively based sensing and monitoring system for IoT", *International Conference on Computer Communication and Informatics (ICCCI)*, 2015, pp. 1-6 Coimbatore, India.
[http://dx.doi.org/10.1109/ICCCI.2015.7218144]

[109] K. Grgić, I. Špeh, and I. Heđi, "A web-based IoT solution for monitoring data using MQTT protocol", *International Conference on Smart Systems and Technologies (SST)*, 2016, pp. 249-253 Osijek, Croatia.
[http://dx.doi.org/10.1109/SST.2016.7765668]

[110] H. Mora, D. Gil, R.M. Terol, J. Azorín, and J. Szymanski, "An IoT-based computational framework for healthcare monitoring in mobile environments", *Sensors (Basel)*, vol. 17, no. 10, p. 2302, 2017.
[http://dx.doi.org/10.3390/s17102302] [PMID: 28994743]

[111] C. Cambra, S. Sendra, J. Lloret, and L. Garcia, "An IoT service-oriented system for agriculture monitoring", *IEEE International Conference on Communications (ICC)*, 2017, pp. 1-6 Paris, France.
[http://dx.doi.org/10.1109/ICC.2017.7996640]

[112] B. Kang, S. Park, T. Lee, and S. Park, "IoT-based monitoring system using tri-level context making model for smart home services", *International Conference on Consumer Electronics (ICCE)*, 2015, pp. 198-199 Las Vegas, NV, USA.

[113] J. Ruan, and Y. Shi, "Monitoring and assessing fruit freshness in IOT-based e-commerce delivery using scenario analysis and interval number approaches", *Inf. Sci.*, vol. 373, pp. 557-570, 2016.
[http://dx.doi.org/10.1016/j.ins.2016.07.014]

[114] N. Ambika, and G.T. Raju, "ECAWSN: eliminating compromised node with the help of auxiliary nodes in wireless sensor network", *Int. J. Sec. Net.*, vol. 9, no. 2, pp. 78-84, 2014.
[http://dx.doi.org/10.1504/IJSN.2014.060743]

[115] N. Ambika, and G.T. Raju, "MA WSN—Manifold authentication in wireless sensor network", *World Congress on Information and Communication Technologies*, 2012, pp. 572-576 Trivandrum, India.
[http://dx.doi.org/10.1109/WICT.2012.6409142]

[116] D.G. Padmavathi, and M. Shanmugapriya, "A survey of attacks, security mechanisms and challenges in wireless sensor networks", *Int. J. Comput. Sci. Inf. Secur.*, vol. 4, no. 1-2, pp. 1-9, 2009.

[117] C. Karlof, N. Sastry, and D. Wagner, "TinySec: a link layer security architecture for wireless sensor networks", In: *2nd international conference on Embedded networked sensor systems*, Baltimore, MD, USA, 2004, pp. 162-175.
[http://dx.doi.org/10.1145/1031495.1031515]

[118] Y. Zhang, W. Liu, W. Lou, and Y. Fang, "Location-based compromise-tolerant security mechanisms for wireless sensor networks", *IEEE J. Sel. Areas Comm.*, vol. 24, no. 2, pp. 247-260, 2006.
[http://dx.doi.org/10.1109/JSAC.2005.861382]

[119] "On communication security in wireless ad-hoc sensor networks", In: *IEEE International Workshops on Enabling Technologies: Infrastructure for Collaborative Enterprises*, Pittsburgh, PA, USA, pp. 139-144, 2002.

[120] H. Yang, F. Ye, Y. Yuan, S. Lu, and W. Arbaugh, "Toward resilient security in wireless sensor networks", In: *6th ACM international symposium on Mobile ad hoc networking and computing*, Urbana-Champaign, IL, USA, 2005, pp. 34-45.
[http://dx.doi.org/10.1145/1062689.1062696]

[121] M.K. Khan, and K. Alghathbar, "Cryptanalysis and security improvements of 'two-factor user authentication in wireless sensor networks'", *Sensors (Basel)*, vol. 10, no. 3, pp. 2450-2459, 2010.
[http://dx.doi.org/10.3390/s100302450] [PMID: 22294935]

[122] M.L. Das, "Two-factor user authentication in wireless sensor networks", *IEEE Trans. Wirel. Commun.*, vol. 8, no. 3, pp. 1086-1090, 2009.

[http://dx.doi.org/10.1109/TWC.2008.080128]

[123] K. Ren, W. Lou, and Y. Zhang, "LEDS: Providing location-aware end-to-end data security in wireless sensor networks", *IEEE Trans. Mobile Comput.,* vol. 7, no. 5, pp. 585-598, 2008.
[http://dx.doi.org/10.1109/TMC.2007.70753]

[124] T. Park, and K.G. Shin, "LiSP: A lightweight security protocol for wireless sensor networks", *ACM Trans. Embed. Comput. Syst.,* vol. 3, no. 3, pp. 634-660, 2004.
[http://dx.doi.org/10.1145/1015047.1015056]

[125] A.C. Ferreira, "On the security of cluster-based communication protocols for wireless sensor networks", *International Conference on Networking,* 2005, pp. 449-458 Reunion Island, France.
[http://dx.doi.org/10.1007/978-3-540-31956-6_53]

[126] H. Cam, S. Ozdemir, P. Nair, and D. Muthuavinashiappan, "ESPDA: energy-efficient and secure pattern-based data aggregation for wireless sensor networks", In: *IEEE Sensors* vol. 2. , 2003, pp. 732-736.
[http://dx.doi.org/10.1109/ICSENS.2003.1279038]

[127] Y. Zhiying, Y. Doh, S. J. Kim, C. S. Pyo, and J. S Chae, "Wireless sensor network and adaptive method for monitoring the security thereof", *Software 8,116,243.,* february 14, 2012.

[128] Y.K. Hsiao, and R.J. Hwang, "An efficient secure data dissemination scheme for grid structure Wireless Sensor Networks", *Int. J. Sec. Net.,* vol. 5, no. 1, pp. 26-34, 2010.
[http://dx.doi.org/10.1504/IJSN.2010.030720]

[129] G. Thamilarasu, "iDetect: an intelligent intrusion detection system for wireless body area networks", *Int. J. Sec. Net.,* vol. 11, no. 1-2, pp. 82-93, 2016.
[http://dx.doi.org/10.1504/IJSN.2016.075074]

[130] Q. Zhang, Y. Tan, L. Zhang, and R. Wang, "A combined key management scheme in wireless sensor networks", *Sens. Lett.,* vol. 9, no. 4, pp. 1501-1506, 2011.
[http://dx.doi.org/10.1166/sl.2011.1671]

[131] F.S. Ouada, M. Omar, A. Bouabdallah, and A. Tari, "Lightweight identity-based authentication protocol for wireless sensor networks", *Int. J. Inform. Comput. Secur.,* vol. 8, no. 2, pp. 121-138, 2016.
[http://dx.doi.org/10.1504/IJICS.2016.078123]

[132] Z. Song, and C. R. Sastry, "Passive RF energy harvesting scheme for wireless sensor", *Software 8, 552, 597,* October 8, 2013.

[133] J. Zhang, J. Tang, T. Wang, and F. Chen, "Energy-efficient data-gathering rendezvous algorithms with mobile sinks for wireless sensor networks", *Int. J. Sen. Net.,* vol. 23, no. 4, pp. 248-257, 2017.
[http://dx.doi.org/10.1504/IJSNET.2017.083533]

[134] M. Dhivya, and M. Sundarambal, "Cuckoo search for data gathering in wireless sensor networks", *IJMC,* vol. 9, no. 6, pp. 642-656, 2011.
[http://dx.doi.org/10.1504/IJMC.2011.042781]

[135] D. Kumar, T.C. Aseri, and R.B. Patel, "Multi-hop communication routing (MCR) protocol for heterogeneous wireless sensor networks", *Int. J. Inf. Techn. Comm. Conver.,* vol. 1, no. 2, pp. 130-145, 2011.
[http://dx.doi.org/10.1504/IJITCC.2011.039281]

[136] J. Tan, "An adaptive collection scheme-based matrix completion for data gathering in energy-harvesting wireless sensor networks", *IEEE Access,* vol. 7, pp. 6703-6723, 2019.
[http://dx.doi.org/10.1109/ACCESS.2019.2890862]

[137] V.C. Gungor, "Efficient available energy monitoring in wireless sensor networks", *Int. J. Sen. Net.,* vol. 3, no. 1, pp. 25-32, 2008.
[http://dx.doi.org/10.1504/IJSNET.2008.016459]

[138] X. Xia, and Q. Liang, "Latency-aware and energy efficiency tradeoffs for wireless sensor networks",

Int. J. Sen. Net., vol. 8, no. 1, pp. 1-7, 2010.
[http://dx.doi.org/10.1504/IJSNET.2010.034062]

[139] B. Elbhiri, R. Saadane, and D. Aboutajdine, "Stochastic and Equitable Distributed Energy-Efficient Clustering (SEDEEC) for heterogeneous wireless sensor networks", *Int. J. Ad Hoc Ubiquitous Comput.,* vol. 7, no. 1, pp. 4-11, 2011.
[http://dx.doi.org/10.1504/IJAHUC.2011.037849]

[140] O. Zytoune, M. El Aroussi, and D. Aboutajdine, "An energy efficient clustering protocol for routing in Wireless Sensor Network", *Int. J. Ad Hoc Ubiquitous Comput.,* vol. 7, no. 1, pp. 54-59, 2011.
[http://dx.doi.org/10.1504/IJAHUC.2011.037853]

[141] R. Roman, C. Alcaraz, and J. Lopez, "A survey of cryptographic primitives and implementations for hardware-constrained sensor network nodes", *Mob. Netw. Appl.,* vol. 12, no. 4, pp. 231-244, 2007.
[http://dx.doi.org/10.1007/s11036-007-0024-2]

[142] E. Lattanzi, and A. Bogliolo, "Hardware filtering of non-intended frames for energy optimisation in wireless sensor networks", *Int. J. Sen. Net.,* vol. 15, no. 2, pp. 121-129, 2014.
[http://dx.doi.org/10.1504/IJSNET.2014.060725]

[143] A. Sabata, and S. Brossia, "Hardware filtering of non–intended frames for energy optimisation in wireless sensor networks", *Int. J. Sen. Net.,* vol. 15, no. 2, pp. 121-129, April 2014.

[144] C. Song, "Maximizing network lifetime based on transmission range adjustment in wireless sensor networks", *Comput. Commun.,* vol. 32, no. 11, pp. 1316-1325, 2009.
[http://dx.doi.org/10.1016/j.comcom.2009.02.002]

[145] S.R. Chatterjee, J. Chowdhury, and M. Chakraborty, "Hardware Realization of Power Adaptation Technique for Cognitive Radio Sensor Node", In: *International Ethical Hacking Conference 2018,* Kolkata, India, 2019, pp. 189-198.
[http://dx.doi.org/10.1007/978-981-13-1544-2_16]

[146] H. Suo, J. Wan, L. Huang, and C. Zou, "Issues and challenges of wireless sensor networks localization in emerging applications", *International Conference on Computer Science and Electronics Engineering,* 2012, pp. 447-451 Hangzhou, China.
[http://dx.doi.org/10.1109/ICCSEE.2012.44]

[147] J. Wang, R.K. Ghosh, and S.K. Das, "A survey on sensor localization", *J. Cont. The. App.,* vol. 8, no. 1, pp. 2-11, 2010.
[http://dx.doi.org/10.1007/s11768-010-9187-7]

[148] P. Biswas, and Y. Ye, "Semidefinite programming for ad hoc wireless sensor network localization", In: *3rd international symposium on Information processing in sensor networks,* Berkeley, California, USA, 2004, pp. 46-54.
[http://dx.doi.org/10.1145/984622.984630]

[149] A.M-C. So, and Y. Ye, "Theory of semidefinite programming for sensor network localization", *Math. Program.,* vol. 109, no. 2-3, pp. 367-384, 2007.
[http://dx.doi.org/10.1007/s10107-006-0040-1]

[150] P. Biswas, T.C. Liang, K.C. Toh, Y. Ye, and T.C. Wang, "Semidefinite programming approaches for sensor network localization with noisy distance measurements", *IEEE Trans. Autom. Sci. Eng.,* vol. 3, no. 4, pp. 360-371, 2006.
[http://dx.doi.org/10.1109/TASE.2006.877401]

[151] A. Vempaty, O. Ozdemir, K. Agrawal, H. Chen, and P.K. Varshney, "Localization in wireless sensor networks: Byzantines and mitigation techniques", *IEEE Trans. Signal Process.,* vol. 61, no. 6, pp. 1495-1508, 2012.
[http://dx.doi.org/10.1109/TSP.2012.2236325]

[152] G. Mao, B.D. Anderson, and B. Fidan, "Path loss exponent estimation for wireless sensor network localization", *Comput. Netw.,* vol. 51, no. 10, pp. 2467-2483, 2007.

[http://dx.doi.org/10.1016/j.comnet.2006.11.007]

[153] C.C. Pu, S.Y. Lim, and P.C. Ooi, "Measurement arrangement for the estimation of path loss exponent in wireless sensor network", *7th International Conference on Computing and Convergence Technology (ICCCT)*, 2012, pp. 807-812 Seoul, South Korea.

[154] N. Saeed, T.Y. Al-Naffouri, and M.S. Alouini, "Outlier detection and optimal anchor placement for 3-D underwater optical wireless sensor network localization", *IEEE Trans. Commun.*, vol. 67, no. 1, pp. 611-622, 2018.
[http://dx.doi.org/10.1109/TCOMM.2018.2875083]

[155] I. Strumberger, M. Beko, M. Tuba, M. Minovic, and N. Bacanin, "Elephant herding optimization algorithm for wireless sensor network localization problem", *Doctoral Conference on Computing, Electrical and Industrial Systems,* 2018, pp. 175-184 Costa de Caparica, Portugal.
[http://dx.doi.org/10.1007/978-3-319-78574-5_17]

[156] X. Zhou, P. Shi, C.C. Lim, C. Yang, and W. Gui, "A dynamic state transition algorithm with application to sensor network localization", *Neurocomputing,* vol. 273, pp. 237-250, 2018.
[http://dx.doi.org/10.1016/j.neucom.2017.08.010]

[157] E. Tuba, M. Tuba, and M. Beko, "Two stage wireless sensor node localization using firefly algorithm", *Smart Trends in Systems, Security and Sustainability,* vol. 18, pp. 113-120, December 2018.
[http://dx.doi.org/10.1007/978-981-10-6916-1_10]

[158] W. J. Kaiser, L. F. Newberg, and G. J. Pottie, "Autonomous tracking wireless imaging sensor network including an articulating sensor and automatically organizing network nodes", *Software 7,305,467,* December 4, 2007.

[159] S. Phoemphon, C. So-In, and D.T. Niyato, "A hybrid model using fuzzy logic and an extreme learning machine with vector particle swarm optimization for wireless sensor network localization", *Appl. Soft Comput.*, vol. 65, pp. 101-120, 2018.
[http://dx.doi.org/10.1016/j:asoc.2018.01.004]

[160] H. A. Cunningham, "Sensor localization using lateral inhibition", *Software 7, 783, 457,* August 24, 2010.

[161] J. J. Park, H. Jeong, S. S. Joo, and J. S. Chae, "Sensor node having self localization function and self localization method thereof", *Software 8, 462, 697,* June 11, 2013.

[162] A. Ali, Y. Ming, S. Chakraborty, and S. Iram, "A comprehensive survey on real-time applications of WSN", *Future internet,* vol. 9, no. 4, p. 77, November 2017.
[http://dx.doi.org/10.3390/fi9040077]

CHAPTER 2

Introduction to Internet-of-Things (IoT)

Abstract: The sensors are tiny devices used to sense the environment or track any object of interest. These are self-configuring devices aiding by minimizing human efforts. Intelligent sensors aggregate resulting in IoT segments. They convert the present reality variable estimated into a digital information stream for transmission to a gateway. Internet of Things (IoT) applications used for city foundations, plants, or wearables utilize enormous varieties of sensors gathering information to transmit over the Internet to a local, cloud-based, and figuring asset. The chapter details the architecture and working of IoT, applications, use cases, challenges of the technology, and future directions. It also highlights the essence of sensors in building an IoT device.

Keywords: Architecture, Authentication, Challenges of IoT, IoT data, IoT objects, Object identification, Sensor IoT.

INTRODUCTION

Sensors [1, 2] are one key factor in IoT achievement, yet these are not traditional sorts that convert physical factors into electrical signals. They advance into something progressively complex to play out and handle the situation in a better manner. It adds the accompanying properties to proceed as IoT segments. The attributes include ease, physically small, remote operatable, able to validate and identify on their own, low power, powerful, self-indicative and self-recuperating, self-aligning, and information pre-preparing ability.

They are the amalgamations of smaller scale electromechanical frameworks, remote interchanges, and computerized devices. They can detect their condition, perform calculations, and impart the same. The most evident disadvantage of the current WSNs is that they are area explicit and task-situated, custom-fitted for specific applications with next to zero chance of reusing them for more update applications. This procedure is wasteful and prompts repetitive organizations for new inclusion. With the introduction of IoT, future WSN organization has bolstered various practices.

Virtualization is an entrenched idea that permits the reflection of real physical registering assets into coherent units, empowering their productive use by numerous autonomous clients. Various applications will have the option to coincide with the equivalent virtualized WSN. Hence it is a promising procedure for WSN arrangements.

Intelligent sensors [157] as IoT parts convert this present reality variable by estimating a computerized information stream for transmission to a destination. The inherent microchip unit knowledge is employed for different capacity devices. They aid in decreasing the heap on the IoT focal assets progressively. They can likewise detect any creation parameters that begin to float past satisfactory standards and produce alerts in a similar manner [3].

IoT parts are arranged into three classes - sink hubs, passage hubs (Gateway nodes), and IoT administrations. Ordinary sink hubs comprise family apparatuses or sensors watching the physical condition, which have low computational assets, stringent vitality requirements, and restricted correspondence assets. The passage hub fills in as a sensor information aggregator and furnishes availability with other sink hubs and specialist co-ops. The passage hubs have additional processing assets contrasted with the sink hubs and give a substitution to the sink hubs. The IoT gathers information from the different door hubs and gives the required to its client or occasion explicit administrations utilizing a designs interface, notice, or application.

ARCHITECTURE AND WORKING OF IOT

The design is characterized as a system of physical segments and its useful association and arrangement, its working standards and methodology, and the information designs utilized in its activity. IoT design contains an assortment of physical items, sensors, cloud administrations, engineers, actuators, correspondence layers, clients, business layers, and IoT conventions. The commonly used five-layered architecture proposed [4] performs the following functionalities –

• Perception Layer consists of the various kinds of sensors and actuators appended to vehicles, cell phones, and other individual gadgets. The essential duty of the layer is to accumulate data of the automobile, traffic condition, and device. This layer is liable for the electromagnetic change and secure transmission of information to the coordination layer. The significant issues are the assortment and separation of caught data in a productive way as far as cost and vitality are concerned.

- The coordination layer of the design focuses on the virtual general system coordination module for heterogeneous systems. The list includes WAVE, Wi-Fi, 4G/LTE, and satellite systems. The prime duty of this layer is to process the distinctive structure of data obtained from heterogeneous systems and reassemble together.

- The Artificial Intelligence (AI) layer of the design concentrates on the virtual cloud foundation. The technology focuses on the Internet of Vehicles (IoV) and is answerable for putting away, preparing, and breaking down the data obtained from the lower layer and dynamic dependent on the primary examination. It functions as a data of the executive's community where processing and examination methods include Vehicular Cloud Computing (VCC) and Big Data Analysis (BDA), and Expert Systems.

- The application layer of the engineering deals with shrewd applications, running from traffic wellbeing and productivity to mixed media-based information and online utility applications. This layer is capable of offering keen types of assistance to end-clients depending on the astute and primary investigation of prepared data by the AI layer.

- The Business layer handles the operational administration module of the IoV. The significant obligation of this layer is to have foreknowledge procedures for the improvement of plans of action dependent on the application utilization information and measurable investigation of them. Various sorts of examination apparatuses include charts, flowchart, correlation tables, use case outlines. Different obligations of the layer incorporate dynamic identification with monetary speculation and use of assets.

Many authors have suggested different architectures understanding the functionalities of the application. The following section details the frameworks used in their work.

The suggestion [5] is the activity of the proposed engineering, condensing the chance to accomplish security that is progressively effective and adaptable with Software Defined Networks (SDN). A local programming program, the SDN controller, deals with the general system conduct. The control and information planes in these networks undergo decoupling and focus on organization insight. The controller can include, update, and erase stream sections, both responsively in light of bundles and proactively with predefined rules. Likewise, SDN empowers quick response to security dangers, granular traffic separating, and dynamic security sending strategies. The OpenDaylight Controller is used on equivalent interaction. It has full access to the switch, and all controllers have similar guidelines. The creators propose Multiple SDN Controller designs for AdHoc Networks. The interchanges between areas with exceptional controllers are called Border Controllers. These edge controllers need to work with another in collaboration to ensure autonomy in all areas.

Various contributors have designed diverse architecture [7, 8] from three-layered to seven-layered design. The section summarizes the same.

Desai, Sheth, & Anantharam [9] suggested Semantic Web empowered IoT engineering to give interoperability between frameworks. It uses setup correspondence and information models. The Semantic Gateway as Service (SGS) permits interpretation between informing conventions. The suggestion [10] is a QoS design dependent on IoT layered structure. This design sets QoS operators in lower layers. It transmits QoS prerequisites, attempting to ensure consistency, which adequately utilizes the current QoS instruments in each layer. Distributed Internet-like Architecture for Things (DIAT) [6] will beat the vast majority of the obstructions during the enormous time spent on scale development of IoT. It explicitly addresses the heterogeneity of IoT gadgets and empowers the consistent expansion of new devices crosswise over applications. The authors propose a utilization control strategy model to help security and protection in an appropriate domain. The proposed layered design gives different degrees of reflection to handle the issues. Some of the problems include versatility, heterogeneity, security, and interoperability. The proposed engineering combines with intellectual abilities that aid in preliminary leadership and empower mechanized creation. Fig. (**1**) represents the layered architecture of the IoT.

Sharma, Chen, and Park's suggestion [11] is a novel blockchain-based conveyed cloud engineering with a product characterized organization (SDN). It aids in empowering controller fog hubs at the edge of the system to meet the necessary plan standards. The proposed model is an appropriated cloud engineering dependent on the blockchain innovation, which gives minimal effort, security, and on-request access to the most aggressive registering foundations in an IoT organization. By making a dispersed cloud foundation, the proposed model empowers practical superior registering. Besides, to carry processing assets to the edge of the IoT, arrange and permit low dormancy access to a lot of information in a safe way, the creators give a secure fog hub engineering that utilizes SDN and blockchain systems. Fog hubs are conveyed fog registering elements that permit the organization of fog benefits and are framed by various processing assets at the edge of the IoT arrange.

The DistBlockNet model [12] is an IoT design consolidation of the upsides of two rising advancements - SDN and block-chains innovation. Irrefutably, blockchains enable us to have a dispersed shared system where non-sure individuals can associate with one another without confiding themselves. The proposal also includes refreshing a stream rule table utilizing a block-chains strategy. The procedure safely confirms a form of the stream rule table, approves the stream rule table, and downloads the most recent stream rules table for the IoT sending gadgets. The suggestion of Moosavi *et al.* [13] is the design that depends on the testament based DTLS handshake convention [14]. The proposed verification and approval engineering are building up a model IoT-based medical services framework. The model works on a Pandaboard, a TI SmartRF06 board, and WiSMotes. The CC2538 module incorporated into the TI board works as a brilliant passage. The WisMotes work as therapeutic sensor hubs. The brought together designation based engineering utilizes a progressively secure key administration policy between sensor hub and its transit.

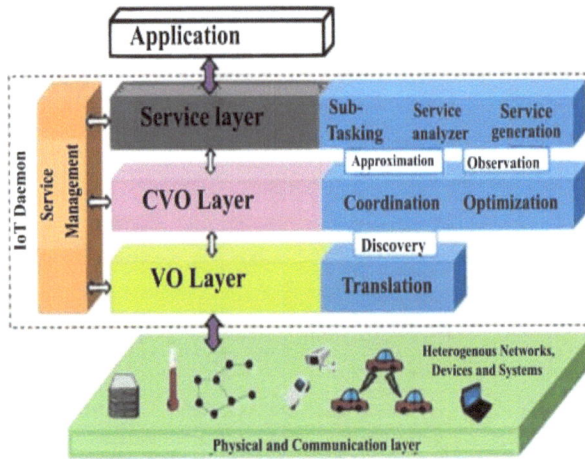

Fig. (1). Layered Architecture of IoT [6].

Another model of IoT engineering [15] joins the advantages of two rising advancements. The list includes programming-characterized systems adminis-tration and fog figuring. The programming-characterized organization suggests an intelligently incorporated system control plane, to permit refined components for traffic control and asset the executives. Catarinucci *et al.* [16] proposed a novel, IoT-aware, brilliant design for programmed checking and following the patients and personnel. The biomedical gadgets embedded inside medical clinics and nursing establishments aid in monitoring. A smart hospital system depends on various, yet correlative advances, explicitly RFID, WSN. It is an intelligent portable system interoperating with one another through a Constrained Application Protocol over low-control remote individual zone organization

(6LoWPAN). The functionality can gather, continuously, both ecological conditions and patients' physiological parameters utilizing an ultra-low-control hybrid sensing network made out of 6LoWPAN hubs coordinating UHF RFID functionalities. Detected information conveys a control focus where a propelled observing application makes them effectively available by both nearby and remote clients through a REST web administration.

Datta, Da Costa, Bonnet, and Härri [17] suggested a proficient MCS empowered IoT system for the savvy urban communities. Co-employable group observation is a combination with an information-driven procedure that gives a uniform instrument to relieve numerous difficulties in urban areas. The structure of the Sancus 2.0 [18] proposal can create and assess a model FPGA execution. The model broadens an MSP430 processor with equipment support for the memory control and cryptographic usefulness required to run the same. The work [19] is the design for IoT administration comprising three layers - the observation layer, the organization layer, and the administration layer. Correspondingly, the system model distinguishes client needs and aids in administration coordination. Web-based business is one of the most significant applications on the Internet. It runs on the organization of data administration.

Misra, Simmhan, and Warrior [20] proposed ten structures designed to accomplish sustainable and pragmatic IoT engineering for India. The standards incorporate Human-driven methodology instead of a thing-driven design. Chen, Tian, Cui, Yin, & Wang [21] reported a trusted design that coordinates the Software-Defined Network (SDN) in IoT. It is a cross-layer approval convention dependent on the proposed model. For a trust foundation, the author's proposal is a Behavior-based Reputation Evaluation Scheme for the Node (BES) and an Organization Reputation Evaluation Scheme (ORES).

The system [22] is a decentralized system using different switches, merchants, and handlers claimed by the network. The design comprises a lot of entryways, switches, and intermediaries. Portals forward the messages they get to at least one router. The dealers confirm the uprightness of the data to anticipate mock gadgets and play out the capacity of the system server portrayed by the LoRaWAN standard. The handler can dispatch the information legitimately to the application. The work [23] incorporates various degrees of IOT administration stages. The super-ordinate IOT administration oversees at least one of the accompanying capacity elements. The IoT terminal entryway, subordinate IoT administration stage, exceptional help stage, and administration door are some of its kind. Table **1** provides the four-layered architecture of IoT.

Table 1. Four layered architecture of IoT [24].

Layers	Description
Sensing layer	The remote frameworks with labels or sensors are currently ready to naturally detect and trade data among various gadgets.
Networking layer	Interfaces everything together and enables things to impart the data to other associated things and amass data from existing IT frameworks.
Service layer	It gives administrations to fulfill client's needs.
Interface layer	It gives communication techniques to clients and different applications.

RESOURCES AND SERVICES OF IOT

IoT Objects

The present reality objects are smart gadgets installed with empowering advances to screen the earth, accumulate information, process it, speak with other IoT items, and take some action. Search frameworks attempt to find these IoT objects dependent on their state data as well as information produced by them. Some hunt frameworks may separate between the IoT articles and their empowering innovations inserted in them.

Chi *et al.* (2014) proposed [25] the strategy to plan a reconfigurable shrewd sensor interface for mechanical WSN in IoT condition. The composite programmable rationale gadget (CPLD) is the central controller. It can peruse data in parallel and include distinctive sensor information. The work uses the standard of the IEEE1451.2 sensor interface. It extensively stipulates the intelligent sensor equipment and programming structure system and relevant interface convention to acknowledge the smart procurement of sensors.

The work [26] is a safe IoT-based brilliant home mechanization framework. The work suggested Triangle Based Security Algorithm (TBSA). The proposed TBSA in the reconciliation of the low power Wi-Fi was remembered for WSNs with the Internet to build up a novel IoT-based intelligent home. The methodology could give secure information transmission among a few related sensor hubs in the system over a long meet range.

IoT Data

The information produced by the IoT items is divided into two kinds (given its relationship to the information source)-

- Observation and Measurement information, information produced by sensors, upgrades to an occasion in a genuine world.

- Context-information gives a depiction of the IoT article's state and its working condition.

The proposal [27] is a new stage configuration used to coordinate new devoted Hardware/Software, which is a piece of information preparing into the in-field gadgets. It will empower the adaptability of the stage by bringing down remote preparing time, with low information transmission and capacity. The phase is separated into three categories- information obtaining, preparing, and capacity perception.

Xu *et al.* [28] suggested to store and translate IoT information. At that point, asset-based information obtained intends to secure and process IoT information pervasively to improve the availability of IoT information assets. An IoT-based framework for crisis restoration administrations aims to gather, incorporate, and interoperate IoT information deftly to offer help to crisis therapeutic administrations. The proposal [29] is a capacity of the executive's arrangement called IOTMDB dependent on NoSQL as present stockpiling arrangements are not well suited for putting away enormous and heterogeneous IoT information.

Use Cases

Many scenarios are under consideration to demonstrate the idea. The section provides a detailed report on test cases suggested by various contributors.

The method [30] allows the protection of IoT devices using robust encryption and authentication means. The constrained devices can benefit from the same security functionalities that are typical to unconstrained domains. These domains have to execute computationally intensive operations. The suggested procedure entails the offloading of some of the computational burden, namely the generation of the master key, from the IoT device on to a suitable (trusted) Gateway node.

The work [31] summarizes the research and development results of IoT studies and discusses the ideas on how to apply them to business. The work focuses on giving a review and examining openings and business prospects of IoT advancements. The progress applies to the territories of medicinal services and the backing to the voyagers. The authors have chosen two zones. The utilization cases are setting ward and are client-driven, where the essential job is to condition and collaborate.

The hut architecture [32] is a simple but scalable architecture for ingesting and analyzing IoT data, which uses historical data analysis to provide context for real-time analysis. The authors implemented a version of the Madrid Traffic use case on the IBM Bluemix platform, together with collaborators from the IBM Bluemix Architecture Center. Bluemix is an IBM PaaS offering, providing micro-services for the main components used in the hut architecture instance.

The proposal [33] examines the capability of UAVs, furnished with IoT gadgets, in conveying IoT administrations from incredible statures. The UAVs (Lagkas, Argyriou, Bibi, & Sarigiannidis, 2018) are swarming observation dependent on face acknowledgment. The offloading of video information handled on the MEC hub contrasted with the neighborhood preparation of video information locally. The authors have built up a testbed comprising a nearby device and one MEC hub. To perform face acknowledgment, the Local Binary Pattern Histogram strategy from the Open Source Computer Vision is utilized. They obtained the outcomes to show the effectiveness of the MEC-based offloading approach in sparing the rare vitality of UAVs. The procedure decreases the handling time of acknowledgment, and speedily distinguishing suspicious people.

Adjih *et al.* [34] suggested the FIT IoT-LAB testbed, an open testbed made out of 2728 low-control remote hubs and 117 versatile robots accessible for trying different things with large scale remote IoT innovations. They are running from low-level conventions to cutting edge Internet administrations. IoT-LAB works to quicken the advancement of tomorrow's IoT innovation by offering an exact open-access and open-source multi-client logical apparatus. Six locales crosswise over France are using IoT-LAB testbed. Each webpage highlights have a distinctive hub and equipment capacities. All locations are interconnected and are accessible through a similar web-based interface, regular REST interfaces, and steady CLI instruments. During the analysis, the robot pursues a circuit exchanging straight lines and turns while going through a hallway. The work highlights the incorporation of restriction calculation with the robot's records. They have a precision superior to 5cm, giving a ground truth to the examination. The authentic direction of the robot and its estimation areas are utilizing the bundle based methodology. Area exactness changes significantly when the robot near hub is m3-30, its essence is identified by eight centers, yielding a restriction precision around 5m. The accuracy is a lot more regrettable toward the finish of the passage, as fewer hubs hear the guides communicating the robot.

Ouerhani, Pazos, Aeberli, & Muller [35] suggested a genuine demonstrated answer for dynamic road light control and the board. The proposal depends on open and adaptable IoT engineering. Considerable commitment is available at the interoperability level utilizing novel gadget association ideas. The thought is dependent on model-driven correspondence specialists to accelerate the reconciliation of sensors and actuators to the Internet of Things stages. The conduct of sensors and actuators is displayed and indicated utilizing XML or JSON design. A java code generator creates to change those determinations into OSGi packs [36]. These packs sent onto a Gateway associate the sensors and the actuators to a focal IoT stage. The OSGi groups guarantee the association and the correspondence with the sensors and the actuators. In the application, remote ecological sensors and nearness locators utilization aids in control pertinent information. A remote Outdoor Light Controller (OLC) is utilized as an actuator to control the force of road lights.

The suggestion [37] is a way to deal with applying the savvy space worldview for communication of various gadgets as data and calculation assets on the interoperability level. The methodology depends on the M3 design for shrewd spaces. M3 represents multiple devices, multiple vendors, and domains. The need is to elevate receptiveness and to concentrate on interoperability. It characterizes proper plan rules that help-

- Interoperability for a large number of heterogeneous devices, services, and users localized in the surrounding.

- Setting awareness, situational and customized administration development and conveyance. The use cases cover application spaces as social organizing, collective work, smart co-ordinations, and e-Tourism.

CHALLENGES

Object Identification

Although the Domain Name System (DNS) gives name interpretation administrations to Internet clients, it is a shaky naming framework. It stays powerless against different assaults. For example, DNS store harming assault and man-in-the-middle assault. This poising assault infuses fake DNS records into people's stores and legitimately bargains the goals mapping between naming design and engineering. Along these lines, without the honesty insurance of the recordings, the whole naming design is uncertain. The section provides a briefing of the security contributions.

The proposal [38] is property-aware name administration. It underpins what, where, and when properties of each IoT object are related to one of a kind, content-based, and intelligible personality assignments. Chun *et al.* [39] suggested an adaptable physical-object naming framework that reuses the current ontologies and appoints URL-based semantic identifiers.

S-URL scheme works in an IoT domain. The authors have executed the models of PONS and IoT object index applications utilizing Apache Web Server, MySQL5, PHP5, and a system of RDF API for PHP. Likewise, relative ideas of different kinds and their examples are created and acquired from the SSN metaphysics.

The work [40] defines strategies, frameworks, and gadgets for recognizable proof and security bootstrapping of a brilliant item inside the improved home condition. The system may incorporate the mechanized tasks of a gadget level ID and security qualification for each smart article in the home utilizing an asset index.

Yan *et al.* [41] recommended the work for the shared name goals in IoT. The system supports the present and future heterogeneous object naming plans. The work utilizes to interpret the significant name to a level string with no semantic importance. The proposal [42] is a chipless RFID tag incorporation with a sensor for IoT application. The tag is fit for transmitting data of 9-piece information. With the adjustment in dielectric permittivity, there will be a move in resonances. The attached tags aid in the observation and detection of dampness.

Authorization and Authentication

The public-key cryptosystems have an advantage for building verification plans or approval frameworks. The absence of a worldwide root authentication authority impedes numerous hypothetically plausible schemes from really being sent. Without the International root Certificate Authority, it turns out to be extremely difficult in testing the structure and validating the framework for IoT. Hence, the idea of designated confirmation and appointed approval ponders over IoT.

Moosavi, *et al.* [13] recommended the design that depended on the authentication based Datagram Transport Layer Security (DTLS) handshake convention [14] as it is the central IP security answer for IoT. The proposed confirmation and approval engineering have tried by building up a model IoT-based human services framework. The model works on a Pandaboard, a TI SmartRF06 board, and WiSMotes. The CC2538 module coordinated into the TI board goes about as a shrewd entryway. The WisMotes go about as medicinal sensor hubs. The proposed engineering is more secure than a best in class unified assignment based design. It utilizes an increasingly safeguard key administration provision between sensor hubs and the keen entryway.

Seitz *et al.* [43] suggested a lot of security and execution necessities for the setting. The approval structure circulating and handling costs between compelled gadgets are less obliged by the back-end servers. The procedure keeps the message trades with the impelled devices at the very least. The configuration [44] depends on OAuth 1.0a, which is an open approval standard for web applications. The plan actualizes on a genuine MQTT-based IoT administration stage.

The work [45] is a productive verification and access control strategy that depends on the general perspective on the security issues for the recognition layer of the IoT. It concentrates on shared confirmation and secure foundation dependent on Elliptic Curve Cryptosystem (ECC). It has a lot of lower stockpiling and correspondence overheads. To get to the control approach, the authors have used the ABAC-based approval technique. The proposal [46] concentrates on a straightforward and constructive secure foundation dependent on ECC. For the entrance control strategy, the authors have suggested RBAC-based (role-based Access Control) approval technique utilizing the thing's specific role and application in the related IoT organization.

FUTURE WORK

As we move towards the future, we look into betterment that provides ease and minimizing human efforts. The system bestows a complete optimized system that embeds positive aspects of various contributions. While designing the entire system, vital concepts consideration is essential. There can be an improvement in the work provided by divergent authors. This section describes the same.

The unwavering quality and the security of the ZigBee organization suggest guaranteeing a sheltered activity of the preliminary foundation of road lighting [35]. Future work can include dynamic road lighting. The contribution [31] prompts the improvement of models for building exceptional tweaked administrations comprising alterable, complimentary modules created by different free suppliers.

REFERENCES

[1]   T. Arampatzis, J. Lygeros, and S. Manesis, "A survey of applications of wireless sensors and wireless sensor networks", *International Symposium on, Mediterrean Conference on Control and Automation Intelligent Control,* 2005, pp. 719-724 Limassol, Cyprus.
      [http://dx.doi.org/10.1109/.2005.1467103]

[2]   H. Meixner, and R. Jones, Sensors, micro-and nanosensor technology: trends in sensor markets, 1st ed., Wolfgang Göpel and J. N. Joachim Hesse, Eds. Hoboken, New Jersey, United States: John Wiley & Sons, 2008, vol. 8.

[3]   Y.Y. Sergey, and M.T.S. Gomes, *Smart Sensors and MEMS.,* S. Nihtianov, A. Luque, Eds., 2nd ed. Sensors: Sawston, United Kingdom, 2005.

[4]   O. Kaiwartya, "Internet of vehicles: Motivation, layered architecture, network model, challenges, and

future aspects", *IEEE Access,* vol. 4, pp. 5356-5373, 2016.
[http://dx.doi.org/10.1109/ACCESS.2016.2603219]

[5]   O. Flauzac, C.J. Gonzalez Santamaría, and F. Nolot, "New security architecture for IoT network", *International Workshop on Big Data and Data Mining Challenges on IoT and Pervasive Systems (BigD2M 2015),* 2015, pp. 1028-1033 London, UK.

[6]   C. Sarkar, "DIAT: A scalable distributed architecture for IoT", *IEEE Internet of Things journal,* vol. 2, no. 3, pp. 230-239, June 2014.

[7]   N.M. Kumar, and P.K. Mallick, "The Internet of Things: Insights into the building blocks, component interactions, and architecture layers", *International Conference on Computational Intelligence and Data Science (ICCIDS 2018),* vol. 132, 2018, pp. 109-117 Gurugram, India.
[http://dx.doi.org/10.1016/j.procs.2018.05.170]

[8]   M. Wu, T.J. Lu, F.Y. Ling, J. Sun, and H.Y. Du, "Research on the architecture of Internet of Things", *3rd International Conference on Advanced Computer Theory and Engineering (ICACTE),* 2010, pp. 484-487 Chengdu, China.

[9]   P. Desai, A. Sheth, and P. Anantharam, "Semantic gateway as a service architecture for iot interoperability", In: *IEEE International Conference on Mobile Services*, New York, NY, USA, 2015, pp. 313-319.
[http://dx.doi.org/10.1109/MobServ.2015.51]

[10]   R. Duan, X. Chen, and T. Xing, "A QoS architecture for IOT", *International Conference on Internet of Things and 4th International Conference on Cyber, Physical and Social Computing,* 2011, pp. 717-720 Dalian, China.

[11]   P.K. Sharma, M.Y. Chen, and J.H. Park, "A software defined fog node based distributed blockchain cloud architecture for IoT", *IEEE Access,* vol. 6, pp. 115-124, 2017.
[http://dx.doi.org/10.1109/ACCESS.2017.2757955]

[12]   P.K. Sharma, S. Singh, Y.S. Jeong, and J.H. Park, "Distblocknet: A distributed blockchains-based secure sdn architecture for iot networks", *IEEE Commun. Mag.,* vol. 55, no. 9, pp. 78-85, 2017.
[http://dx.doi.org/10.1109/MCOM.2017.1700041]

[13]   S.R. Moosavi, "SEA: a secure and efficient authentication and authorization architecture for IoT-based healthcare using smart gateways", *6th International Conference on Ambient Systems, Networks and Technologies (ANT-2015),* 2015, pp. 452-459 London, UK.
[http://dx.doi.org/10.1016/j.procs.2015.05.013]

[14]   "T.'Schmitt, C. Kothmayr, W. Hu, M. Brünig, and G. Carle, "DTLS based security and two-way authentication for the Internet of Things", *Ad Hoc Netw.,* vol. 11, no. 8, pp. 2710-2723, 2013.
[http://dx.doi.org/10.1016/j.adhoc.2013.05.003]

[15]   S. Tomovic, K. Yoshigoe, I. Maljevic, and I. Radusinovic, "Software-defined fog network architecture for IoT", *Wirel. Pers. Commun.,* vol. 92, no. 1, pp. 181-196, 2017.
[http://dx.doi.org/10.1007/s11277-016-3845-0]

[16]   L. Catarinucci, "An IoT-aware architecture for smart healthcare systems", *IEEE Int. Thiings J.,* vol. 2, no. 6, pp. 515-526, 2015.
[http://dx.doi.org/10.1109/JIOT.2015.2417684]

[17]   S.K. Datta, R.P.F. Da Costa, C. Bonnet, and J. Härri, "oneM2M architecture based IoT framework for mobile crowd sensing in smart cities", *European conference on networks and communications (EuCNC),* 2016, pp. 168-173 Athens, Greece.
[http://dx.doi.org/10.1109/EuCNC.2016.7561026]

[18]   J. Noorman, "Sancus 2.0: A low-cost security architecture for IoT devices", *ACM Transactions on Privacy and Security,* vol. 20, no. 3, p. 7, 2017.
[http://dx.doi.org/10.1145/3079763]

[19]   X. Shang, R. Zhang, and Y. Chen, "Internet of things (IoT) service architecture and its application in

e-commerce", *J. Electron. Commerce Organ.,* vol. 10, no. 3, pp. 44-55, 2012.
[http://dx.doi.org/10.4018/jeco.2012070104]

[20]   P. Misra, Y. Simmhan, and J. Warrior, "Towards a practical architecture for internet of things: An india-centric view", *IEEE Internet of Things Newsletter,* pp. 1-2, January 2015.

[21]   J. Chen, Z. Tian, X. Cui, L. Yin, and X. Wang, "Trust architecture and reputation evaluation for internet of things", *J. Ambient Intell. Humaniz. Comput.,* vol. 10, no. 8, pp. 3099-3107, 2019.
[http://dx.doi.org/10.1007/s12652-018-0887-z]

[22]   W. Giezeman, *IoT magazine. [Online].,* January, 2016.   https://iot.ieee.org/newsletter/january-2016/building-a-crowdsourced-global-iot-network-operator.html?source=post_page

[23]   H. Li, and X. Xing, "Internet of things service architecture and method for realizing internet of things service,", *Software 8, 984, 113,* March 17, 2015.

[24]   S. Li, L. Da Xu, and S. Zhao, "The internet of things: a survey", *Inf. Syst. Front.,* vol. 17, no. 2, pp. 243-259, 2015.
[http://dx.doi.org/10.1007/s10796-014-9492-7]

[25]   Q. Chi, H. Yan, C. Zhang, Z. Pang, and L. Da Xu, "A reconfigurable smart sensor interface for industrial WSN in IoT environment", *IEEE Trans. Industr. Inform.,* vol. 10, no. 2, pp. 1417-1425, 2014.
[http://dx.doi.org/10.1109/TII.2014.2306798]

[26]   S. Pirbhulal, H. Zhang, M.E. E Alahi, H. Ghayvat, S.C. Mukhopadhyay, Y.T. Zhang, and W. Wu, "A novel secure IoT-based smart home automation system using a wireless sensor network", *Sensors (Basel),* vol. 17, no. 1, p. 69, 2016.
[http://dx.doi.org/10.3390/s17010069] [PMID: 28042831]

[27]   Y. Nait Malek, "On the use of IoT and Big Data Technologies for Real-time Monitoring and Data Processing", *7th International Conference on Current and Future Trends of Information and Communication Technologies in Healthcare,* vol. 113, 2017, pp. 429-434 Coimbra, Portugal.

[28]   B. Xu, "Ubiquitous data accessing method in IoT-based information system for emergency medical services", *IEEE Trans. Industr. Inform.,* vol. 10, no. 2, pp. 1578-1586, 2014.
[http://dx.doi.org/10.1109/TII.2014.2306382]

[29]   T. Li, Y. Liu, Y. Tian, S. Shen, and W. Mao, "A storage solution for massive iot data based on nosql", *IEEE International Conference on Green Computing and Communications,* 2012, pp. 50-57 Besancon, France.
[http://dx.doi.org/10.1109/GreenCom.2012.18]

[30]   R. Bonetto, "Secure communication for smart IoT objects: Protocol stacks, use cases and practical examples", In: *IEEE international symposium on a world of wireless, mobile and multimedia networks (WoWMoM), San Francisco, CA, USA,* 2012, pp. 1-7.
[http://dx.doi.org/10.1109/WoWMoM.2012.6263790]

[31]   E. Balandina, S. Balandin, Y. Koucheryavy, and D. Mouromtsev, "IoT use cases in healthcare and tourism", In: *IEEE 17th Conference on Business Informatics*, vol. 2, Lisbon, Portugal, 2015, pp. 37-44.
[http://dx.doi.org/10.1109/CBI.2015.16]

[32]   P. Ta-Shma, "An ingestion and analytics architecture for iot applied to smart city use cases", *IEEE Int. Things J.,* vol. 5, no. 2, pp. 765-774, 2017.
[http://dx.doi.org/10.1109/JIOT.2017.2722378]

[33]   N.H. Motlagh, M. Bagaa, and T. Taleb, "UAV-based IoT platform: A crowd surveillance use case", *IEEE Commun. Mag.,* vol. 55, no. 2, pp. 128-134, 2017.
[http://dx.doi.org/10.1109/MCOM.2017.1600587CM]

[34]   C. Adjih, "FIT IoT-LAB: A large scale open experimental IoT testbed", In: *IEEE 2nd World Forum on Internet of Things (WF-IoT)*, Milan, Italy, 2015, pp. 459-464.
[http://dx.doi.org/10.1109/WF-IoT.2015.7389098]

[35]   N. Ouerhani, N. Pazos, M. Aeberli, and M. Muller, "IoT-based dynamic street light control for smart cities use cases", *International Symposium on Networks, Computers and Communications (ISNCC)*, 2016, pp. 1-5 Yasmine Hammamet, Tunisia.
[http://dx.doi.org/10.1109/ISNCC.2016.7746112]

[36]   M. Stusek, "Performance analysis of the OSGi-based IoT frameworks on restricted devices as enablers for connected-home", *7th International Congress on Ultra Modern Telecommunications and Control Systems and Workshops (ICUMT)*, 2015, pp. 178-183 Brno, Czech Republic.
[http://dx.doi.org/10.1109/ICUMT.2015.7382424]

[37]   D.G. Korzun, S.I. Balandin, A.M. Kashevnik, A.V. Smirnov, and A.V. Gurtov, "Smart spaces-based application development: M3 architecture, design principles, use cases, and evaluation", *Int. J. Embed. Real-Time Commun. Syst.*, vol. 8, no. 2, pp. 66-100, 2017.
[http://dx.doi.org/10.4018/IJERTCS.2017070104]

[38]   Z. K. Zhang, M. C. Y. Cho, Z. Y. Wu, and S. W. Shieh, "Identifying and Authenticating IoT Objects in a Natural Context", *IEEE computer*, vol. 48, no. 8, pp. 81-83, August 2015.
[http://dx.doi.org/10.1109/MC.2015.213]

[39]   S. Chun, J. Jung, X. Jin, G. Cho, and K.H. Lee, "Semantically enriched object identification for Internet of Things", *International Conference on Distributed Computing in Sensor Systems*, 2014, pp. 141-142 Marina Del Rey, CA, USA.

[40]   S. A. Rahman, D. N. Seed, L. Dong, C. Wang, and Q. Ly, "Smart object identification in the digital home", *Software 10, 256, 982*, April 9, 2019.

[41]   Z. Yan, N. Kong, Y. Tian, and Y.J. Park, "A universal object name resolution scheme for IoT", *International Conference on Green Computing and Communications and IEEE Internet of Things and IEEE Cyber, Physical and Social Computing*, 2013, pp. 1120-1124 Beijing, China.
[http://dx.doi.org/10.1109/GreenCom-iThings-CPSCom.2013.193]

[42]   A. Habib, M.A. Azam, Y. Amin, and H. Tenhunen, "Chipless slot resonators for IoT system identification", *IEEE International Conference on Electro Information Technology (EIT)*, 2016, Grand Forks, ND, USA.
[http://dx.doi.org/10.1109/EIT.2016.7535262]

[43]   L. Seitz, G. Selander, and C. Gehrmann, "Authorization framework for the internet-of-things", *14th International Symposium on" A World of Wireless, Mobile and Multimedia Networks"(WoWMoM)*, 2013, pp. 1-6 Madrid, Spain.

[44]   A. Niruntasukrat, "Authorization mechanism for mqtt-based internet of things", *International Conference on Communications Workshops (ICC)*, 2016, pp. 290-295 Kuala Lumpur, Malaysia.
[http://dx.doi.org/10.1109/ICCW.2016.7503802]

[45]   N. Ye, Y. Zhu, R.C. Wang, R. Malekian, and L. Qiao-Min, "An efficient authentication and access control scheme for perception layer of internet of things", *Appl. Math. Inf. Sci.*, vol. 8, no. 4, p. 1617, 2014.
[http://dx.doi.org/10.12785/amis/080416]

[46]   J. Liu, Y. Xiao, and C.P. Chen, "Authentication and access control in the internet of things", *32nd International Conference on Distributed Computing Systems Workshops*, 2012, pp. 588-592 Macau, China.
[http://dx.doi.org/10.1109/ICDCSW.2012.23]

CHAPTER 3

Mobile Cloud Computing

Abstract: Mobile cloud computing (MCC) is the administrations of distributed computing. The facilitation is available to a cell phone or any hand-versatile framework. Portable processing coordinates with distributed computing on account of the fundamental attributes of the cloud model. Some examples include on-request self-administration, asset pooling, quick flexibility, and estimated administrations. Portable Sensor-cloud collects the readings in an unsupervised environment and provides the queried data to the respective clients. This chapter provides a vision into the taxonomy of the mobile cloud system, its security issues, management issues, advantages, applications, challenges, and future directions.

Keywords: Benefits, Mobile cloud computing, Security, Taxonomy.

INTRODUCTION

Distributed computing, termed cloud computing, is another universal technology offering assets register facility. Some examples include functionalities, such as file handling, handling memory, and capacity. These components are not physically in the client's area. A specialist cooperation process deals with these assets that are employed using the Internet. With the help of portable applications and Cloud computing, an assortment of administrations for versatile clients has evolved. Mobile cloud computing is the coordination of Cloud computing in a flexible environment. Mobile clients amass rich experience of different administrations from versatile applications, which run on the gadgets as well as on remote servers through the isolated systems. Lately, the procedure focused on cell phones has begun getting inexhaustible with applications in different classes. Some examples include amusement, games, business, informal communication, travel, and news. Fig. (**1**) represents the reference model of MCC.

TAXONOMY OF MOBILE COMPUTING

The authors have considered the hardware and the software distribution of Mobile cloud computing (MCC) while suggesting the taxonomy of the system.

Ambika Nagaraj

MCC paradigm is differentiated based on four aspects- computation offloading, Multitier programming, live cloud streaming, and remote data managing. Fig. (**2**) represents the taxonomy of MCC.

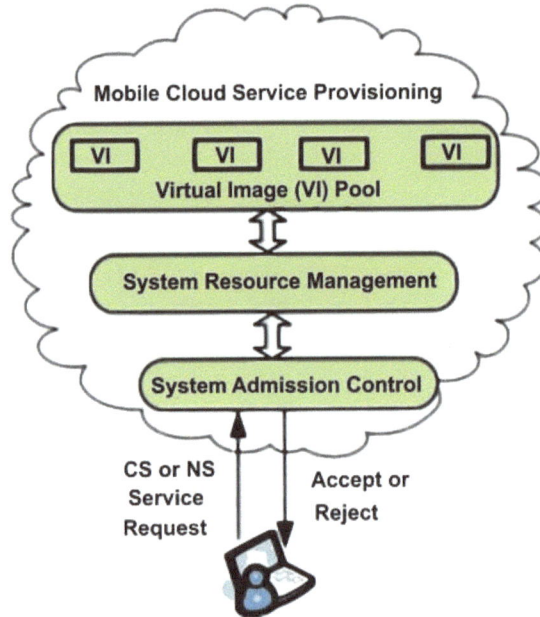

Fig. (1). Reference model for Mobile cloud computing [1].

Computation Offloading

Computation offloading [2] is a process of recognizing, parceling, and relocating parts of portable applications to cloud-based assets. Parceling can occur using three distinct methodologies, which are static, dynamic, and hybrid. The section consists of some of the suggestions provided by various authors.

The creators propose a game-theoretic methodology [3] for accomplishing efficient calculation offloading for portable distributed computing. They suggest the decentralized offloading calculation method by assuming primary leadership issues among cell phone clients as a decentralized calculation offloading game. They have also proposed a decentralized calculation offloading component that can accomplish the Nash harmony of the game [4]. The creators have considered 20 cell phone clients in their work. This instrument dispersion is haphazard over a 50m×50m locale and the remote access base-station in the focal point of the environment. The channel transfer speed is 5 MHz, the transmission power is 100 mwatts, and the foundation commotion is 100 dBm.

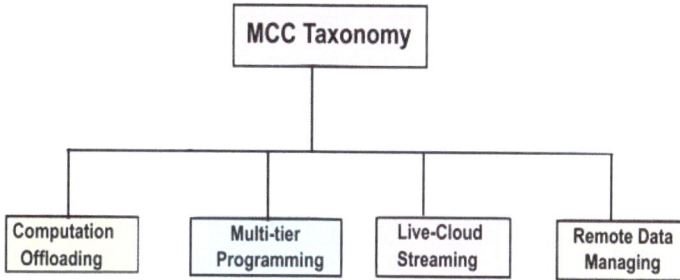

Fig. (2). Taxonomy of MCC.

Chen *et al.* (2015) considered the offloading computation of primary leadership issues among different cell phone clients [5]. The usage of portable edge distributed computing in a multi-channel remote condition as a multi-client calculation offloading game. The creators propose a circulated computation offloading calculation that accomplishes the Nash equilibrium of the game [6]. They have adopted a game-theoretic way to deal with the same.

Huang *et al.* (2012) suggested a versatile offloading calculation that can offload some portion of an application calculation to a devoted server powerfully as indicated by the difference in remote conditions [7]. The proposed calculation depends on the Lyapunov enhancement [8].

Deng *et al.* (2014) [9] suggest a novel offloading framework to structure efficient offloading choices for versatile administrations [11]. The methodology considers the reliance relations among part administrations and enhances execution time and vitality to execute versatile administrations. The suggestion is a genetic algorithm (GA) [10] based offloading technique and execution after cautiously adjusting pieces of a nonexclusive GA. It coordinates the exceptional requirements for the expressed issue.

Kovachev *et al.*, (2012) suggested a mix with the built-up Android application model for the improvement of "off laudable" applications [11]. It is a light-weight application for parceling and consistent, versatile calculation offloading. They have proposed Mobile Augmentation Cloud Services (MACS), an administration's based portable distributed computing middleware. Android applications utilize the MACS middleware, taking advantage of consistent offloading of calculation. MACS structure with two use-case telephone applications consideration enhances the work. The primary process actualizes the N-Queens issue. The subsequent procedure includes face location and acknowledgment in video documents. A Motorola Milestone cell phone that depends on Android stage 2.2 is utilized in the assessment.

Multitier Programming

The MCC innovation presents unconventional testing necessities in the advancement of appropriated programming frameworks-

- The new specialists can leave and land whenever and can meander crosswise over various conditions. The applications must be versatile and fit for managing such changes in an adaptable and solo manner.

- The exercises of the product frameworks are regularly logical, *i.e.*, carefully identified with the platform in which the procedure executes.

- The adherence to the above prerequisites must not conflict with the need for advancement of the preliminary programming model conceivably requiring light supporting foundations.

Mamei & Zambonelli (2004) suggested the programming model of TOTA (ìTuples On the Airî) [12]. It is a novel middleware for supporting versatile setting aware application in unavoidable processing situations. The primary thought in TOTA depends on spatially conveyed tuples, spread over a system. It is based on application-explicit standards, for both logical data and supporting uncoupled collaborations between application segments.

McCann & Roman (1998) [13] suggested UNITY. It is a state-based formalism with an establishment in the transient rationale that simultaneously addresses portable frameworks. Fernando *et al.*, (2012) proposed a group processing structure for cell phones [14]. Honeybee empowers cell phones to share work, use nearby assets, and human-coordinated effort in the versatile setting. It utilizes 'work taking' methodology to viably stack balance errands crosswise over different centers that are from the earlier obscure. Five Android gadgets of shifting abilities, including Nexus S, Ideos, and Galaxy SII, execute the work.

According to Welling & Badrinath (1995), Mobjects are a piece of an item framework [15]. These items present a theoretical perspective on the portable condition and perform primary errands at the programming language level. By exemplifying the versatility impacts inside an item, the working framework interface avoids a portable application engineer.

Live-Cloud Streaming

Live cloud streaming is another methodology that expects to increase cell phones' working by playing out the whole calculations outside the cell phone. The clients receive the results as a pre-arranged screen. This methodology requires low inertness, high throughput, and a dependable remote system.

The suggestion is a cloud-assisted uninterrupted transcoding component [16]. It contains HTTP live drop convention, a coding-mode progress state machine, and three transmission capacity assessments. In the proposal, the fluctuation in the current system is seen by the transfer speed assessment results. If different transcoding procedures utilization in various modes, the proper media fragment bit rate can be determined. It is transcoded into the section to meet the present data transfer capacity conditions. The methodology causes the clients to acquire suitable medium quality, naturally through the HTTP redirection method. Utilizing distributed computing, the client will take various translating media cuts into differing translators indicated by the client's needs. The technique utilization is an innovation to build interpretation proficiency to accomplish constant transcribe. The peak signal-to-noise ratio (PSNR) and transmission capacity undergo division as the reference list of progress in media quality.

Intelligent Mobile Live Video Learning System in a Cloud Environment manages the structure and usage of intuitive learning through cell phones [17]. The facility includes hearing the live talks while catching from the educator webcam. These functionalities are divided into pieces and undergo spilling on the cloud. When a solicitation is obtained from the understudy, live video from the cloud is supported in cell phone nearby memory. It is let out from that point to see the doings. The users can likewise post questions and get an answer from educators through the collaboration offices given.

Xi & Zhang (2014) suggested improving the Dynamic Adaptive Streaming over HTTP (DASH) administration [18]. The indication by the gathered transmission capacity of the gadget follows processing and transcoding. During the assembly stage, the methodology isolates the transcoded stream into pieces for every gadget. After the devices received the sections, each gadget can get the entire portion by trading the parts through the free short-run D2D interface. The work uses Android and a Linux server. It incorporates Sony LT22i and Samsung GT-I9100 and has eight Intel Xeon E5-1620 CPU and 16GB RAM. It uses CentOS.

Garcia-Pineda *et al*. (2016) suggested a few target video quality measurements to assess the emotional Mean Opinion Score (MOS) [19]. The users have to gather broad insights and factors for different framework parameters and apply a Factor Analysis measurement (FA). The authors have actualized a video customer and a spilling server in various VMs. The device used to stream the video has been Video Tester that permits video transmission with RTP over UDP unicast. These recordings have a Common Intermediate Format, 352x288 goals, and coding with three different piece rates as 256 kbps, 512 kbps, and 768 kbps utilizing the codec, H.264/AVC with the accompanying coding choices of 25 casings for each second, profile Main@L1.3 and a GOP size of 50 edges. Chen, Zhang, Wang, & Liu suggested a nonexclusive structure that encourages a practical cloud administration for publicly supported live communication [20]. The cloud servers can be provisioned in a fine granularity to suit Geo-conveyed video crowdsourcers.

Remote Data Managing

Remote Data Managing arrangements, for example, the dropbox, extend versatile stockpiling by putting away clients' advanced substance in the cloud-based assets. Parallel to development in figuring, computerized information is expanding that request in enormous space on cell phones. It further hinders cell phone appropriation and ease of use. The cloud stockpiles upgrade stockpiling inadequacy of cell phones and improve information wellbeing, trust, and information security.

Landis *et al*. (1996) [21] suggested a proposal for accommodation overseeing information move between figuring gadgets. A message recognizes a specific informational collection and a customer profile. When the required information collection maps to the total information collection, the process undergoes affirmation. At the point when the specific gathering does not communicate to the entire assembly, the customer profile usage decides if to transmit extra information to finish the particular informational index, or whether to transmit the total informative collection to supplant the specific informative index.

Todeschini *et al*. (2016) [22] suggested a methodology where the client may finish the structure to make a case of the frame and characterize an occasion appropriation list. The occurrence undertakes dispersion to clients corresponding to the appropriation list as the owner of the structure may likewise adjust the formation. These alterations are additionally consequently disseminated to the clients at the third center. The process initiates a subsequent arrangement connected to the structure and appropriated to the third center also.

Jackson, 1998 [23] suggested a versatile registering gadget empowered by an adjustable information cognizance layer (DCL) programming project. This project changes the data from an assortment of sensors into continuous relevant messages. The DCL programming fuses adaptable programming parts known as modules to extend the utilization of the versatile registering gadget.

Kimchi *et al.* (2015) [24] proposed a cross gadget application programming interface (API). This interface actualizes as a gadget bunch API where the customer executes on the registering gadget. Every gadget bunch API customer incorporates an authorizations module that arranges to decide if a solicitation fulfills a gadget bunch. The explicit consent for access to information put away on any gadget related to the gadget gathering. Endless supply of the solicitation, a record stockpiling module is designed to recover and yield the mentioned document.

Mehmood *et al.* (2014) [25] suggested a tele-endoscopy administration that chooses keyframes dependent on their pertinence to the problem finding. It guarantees the sending of relevant important edges to the gastroenterologist. The methodology excludes transmission expenses and data transfer capacity. The proposed system spares stockpiling costs just as the valuable time of specialists in perusing patient's data.

Welingkar & Nair (2013) [26] suggested a portable figuring gadget that contains a remote handset designed to speak with a remote server, a memory, and a handling circuit. The handling circuit is designed in a reestablish activity to get first information from the remote server, to get a source marker as the second information from the remote server. The primary information and second information communicate information recently put away in the memory of the versatile processing gadget or a memory of another portable figuring gadget. They send a solicitation for the subsequent information dependent on the source pointer utilizing the remote handset.

Sobel & Hernacki (2013) [27] suggested a PC executed technique for safely overseeing interactive media information caught by a portable processing gadget. The technique contains –

- Distinguishing interactive media information caught by the versatile processing gadget.

- Identifying an uneven open key put away on the portable figuring gadget that is related to an unbalanced private key put away on a server.

- Scrambling the sight and sound information utilizing the public key so that the encoded mixed media information undergoes disordering using the private key it is put away on the server.

- Transmitting the encoded varied media information to the server. Fig. (**3**) represents the MCC ecosystem & its players.

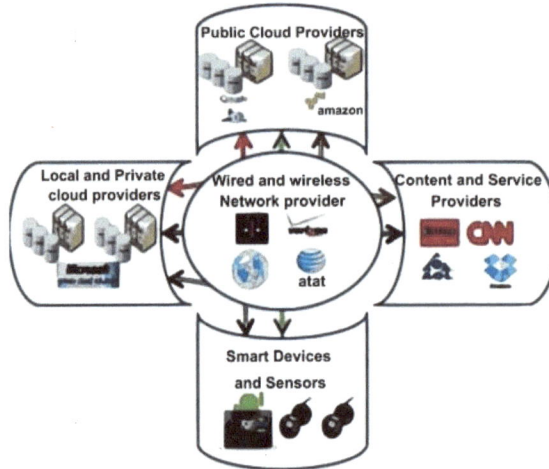

Fig. (3). MCC ecosystem and its players [28].

MOBILE CLOUD SECURITY

At present, cell phones and tablets utilization as a customary phone is trending. The employment in messaging, web perusing, running enormous scope of uses, record sharing, altering reports, engaging, and so on. One of the issues faced by this technology is security. The section details various contributions made by divergent contributors to secure the system.

Huang *et al.* (2010) [29] suggested another versatile cloud structure called MobiCloud. Apart from supporting traditional calculation administrations, MobiCloud additionally upgrades the activity of the specially appointed system. The MobiCloud system will improve correspondence by tending to confide in the board by the secure direction of credentials.

The framework [1] is a Security Service Admission Model (SSAM) that assumes the Semi-Markov Decision Process to display the structure for the cloud supplier. The authors characterize the structure into states by a tuple. Their properties include quantities of clients and related security administration classifications.

They determine the enduring state and management demand blocking likelihood.

The proposal [30] incorporates a registration process designed to such an extent that a gadget might fit inside the submission. The entering may integrate top and base individuals. The procedure removes coupled together to shape the registration. Each top and base part incorporates an edge divide characterized by proximal and distal finishes and rival sides. The top and base individuals may consolidate particular fastening instruments that reach out along the border of the top and base individuals. Its usage in drawing in a third catching component enhances the work. The catching components arrangement for coupling the top and base individuals with each other fixes the lodging.

Peev *et al.* (2006) [31] suggested a versatile processing gadget. The gadget acquires records by introducing on the portable registering gadget based on PC executable guidelines. The guidelines characterize how the documents are to undergo launching on the versatile figuring gadget. The arrangement supervisor at that point causes the PC executable directions execution and causes a reflecting rollback report development. Suppose the establishment falls flat, the establishment procedure switches by executing the rollback report. The arrangement supervisor may likewise utilize to actualize security.

The methodology [32] includes a private data archive kept by the client's confided in specialist and how reliable the client regards disclose. Security includes guaranteeing the exactness of data and the personalities of the communicators. Area data can be untrustworthy in a remote system except if the nonremovable labels undergo pushing. A strategy must be accessible to build up the reliability of the unencountered principals, which could be people, gadgets, or projects. The perfect arrangement is one in which directors and clients have a decision as to how much security implementation payment for some random regulatory space.

Inoue *et al.* (2001) [33] suggested a portable PC and parcel encryption and confirmation strategy that is fit for controlling the actuation of bundle encryption and validation gadget. This instrument is having a place with a versatile PC, indicated by the security arrangement at the visited system of the portable PC. The flexible PC encompasses encryption and verification units having an ON/OFF switchable capacity. Its usage for applying an encryption and verification handling on input bundles of the portable PC enhances the contribution. At that point, one of the bundle encryption and confirmation unit and an outer parcel handling gadget encrypts and verifies the information parcels.

The methodology [34] is a unique mark biometric utilized to client check, secured by a computationally effective Public Key Infrastructure (PKI) scheme, Elliptic Curve Cryptography (ECC). The certified unique finger impression data covers up in the component vault that is the blend of authentic and debris properties. Unique mark attributes are utilized for biometric confirmation as well as for cryptographic keys.

Oberheide *et al.* (2008) [35] suggested a model whereby portable antivirus usefulness is moved to an off-gadget arrange administration. It utilizes various virtualized malware discovery motors. The contention is that it is conceivable to spend data transfer capacity to decrease on-gadget CPU, memory, and power assets.

DATA MANAGEMENT ISSUES

In versatile distributed computing, cell phones [36] can depend on distributed computing and data stockpiling assets to perform computationally concentrated tasks. Despite giving customary calculation administrations, versatile cloud additionally upgrades the activity of conventional impromptu system by regarding cell phones as administration hubs. The detected data is prepared and put away in a safe manner guaranteeing the client's security in the cloud.

Huang *et al.*, (2011) [37] is portable cloud information. It prepares structure using the trust of the board and private data segregation. The dynamic cloud has three primary areas - the cloud versatile and detecting space, the cloud confided in area, and the cloud open help and capacity area. In this structure, every cell phone undergoes virtualization as an Extended Semi-Shadow Images (ESSI) in the cloud confided in the area. The acquainted ESSIs can be utilized with address correspondence and calculation insufficiencies of a cell phone, and give upgraded security and security assurances. A cell phone and its comparing ESSI can likewise act like a specialist organization or a help merchant as indicated by its capacity.

The proposal [38] suggests a novel Privacy-Preserving Cipher Policy Attribute-Based Encryption (PP-CP-ABE). Utilizing PP-CP-ABE, light-weight gadgets can safely re-appropriate considerable encryption and decoding activities to cloud specialist co-ops, without uncovering the information content. Second, they propose an Attribute-Based Data Storage (ABDS) framework as a cryptographic gathering based access control instrument. The work includes a suggestion to assess the presence of these intelligent radio accesses to a specific radio system test system [39].

Jia *et al.*, (2011) [40] suggested a secure mobile user-based data service mechanism (SDSM) to give classification and fine-grained access control for information. This instrument empowers portable clients to appreciate protected re-appropriated information administrations with limited security and board overhead. The versatile cloud specialist co-ops can collaborate to make an asset pool to impart their very own assets to one another. Therefore, the assets can be better used, and it can undergo an expansion of income of the versatile cloud specialist co-ops. To expand the advantage of the portable cloud specialist organizations, the authors propose a system [41] for asset distribution to the versatile applications. For asset assignment to the versatile applications, the suggestion of improvement models to acquire the ideal number of use cases are suggested. The system can amplify the income of the specialist organizations while meeting the asset prerequisites of the portable applications. For sharing the income created from the asset pool among the agreeable portable cloud specialist co-ops in an alliance, the authors apply the ideas of center and Shapley esteem [42] from the game hypothesis. Given the income shares, the versatile cloud specialist organizations can choose whether to collaborate and share the assets in the asset pool or not. Additionally, the supplier can improve the choice of the measure of assets to add to the asset pool.

The work [43] describes the arrangement of human services and portable distributed computing and enormous information investigation in its enablement. A suggestion includes a cloudlet-based versatile distributed computing framework to be utilized for mortal services boundless information applications.

Tawalbeh *et al.*, (2016) [44] proposed an ace cloudlet with the board plan to sort out the correspondence between the cloudlets themselves. Tawalbeh *et al.*, (2016) [45] suggested a productive and secure versatile distributed computing model dependent on the Cloudlet idea. In this system, the cell phones of the clients can interface legitimately to cloud assets utilizing less expensive advances. When required, and just if the administration is not accessible in the cloudlet, the client will be associated with the venture cloud.

ADVANTAGES OF MCC

Storage

The cloud can suit and store considerably more information contrasted with a PC. Utilizing the facility enables access to boundless stockpiling capacity and versatility. In this way, no more framework ventures or time spent includes new servers are necessary. The cloud saves organizations the interest to redesign their PC equipment, further diminishing the general IT cost.

Itani *et al.*, (2010) [46] suggested the convention that applies gradual cryptography ideas. It confides in processing to configuration secure uprightness information structures that ensure the client's information. It profoundly decreases the portable customer vitality utilization and productively supporting robust information tasks.

Ren *et al.*, (2011) [47] concentrated on the capacity re-appropriating in the doubted Cloud server. After a mobile device makes a record, it might transfer the document into numerous cloud servers. Host client or different cooperators may get to it later on distributed. The security and trustworthiness of the record enhance the capacity of cloud servers during the period of transfer. The creators have proposed an encryption-based plan for the circumstance of the single open cloud server. It is a coding-based plan for the situations where various cloud servers are accessible without depending on encryption, sharing based schemes to diminish the calculation overhead by just depending on the activity.

The suggestion [48] is a technique that mutually enhances the transmit control, the number of bits per image, and the CPU cycles doled out to every application. It aims to limit the power utilization at the versatile side, under a typical inactivity imperative directed by the application prerequisites. They have considered a lot of versatile handsets served by a solitary cloud and the enhancement of a balanced connection between the transmit control and the level of CPU cycles availed to every client. The creators propose a calculation planning strategy and check the security of the calculations line. It infers the degrees of the opportunity of the channels between portable handsets and servers.

Flexibility

Distributed computing permits a dynamic versatility system. The cloud is not subject to nearby equipment or programming. Therefore the client increases another degree of adaptability as far as getting to the arrangement.

Mora *et al.*, (2015) [49] suggested a proposition that consolidates loose processing systems with distributed computing standards. It gives flexible execution structures for installation. Subsequently, the uncertain calculation planning technique on the outstanding burden of the implanted framework is the answer. The procedure moves to register the cloud as per the need. Hence the system has the option to meet the profitability and nature of wanted administrations. A method to assess arranges delays and to plan all the more precisely errands is received.

F2AC [50] is a light-weight, fine-grained, and adaptable access control methodology. The procedure documents stockpiling in portable distributed computing. F2AC accomplishes iterative approval, validation with custom-fitted arrangements, and access control for progressively changing getting to gatherings. It also brings to benefit change and disavowal. Another entrance control model called coordinated tree with a connected leaf model is proposed for additional usage in information structures and calculations.

Yan *et al.*, (2015) [51] suggested a plan to control information access in distributed computing. The procedure is dependent on trust assessed by the information proprietor as well as notorieties. These assessors created by various notoriety focuses in an adaptable way by applying Attribute-Based Encryption and Proxy Re-Encryption. Cuckoo [52] is a plan of adaptable register concentrated errand offloading in MCC for vitality sparing. It utilizes a mix of static investigation and dynamic profiling. It focuses on assignments that are fine-grained set apart from disconnected versatile application codes. The creators have proposed a horizon based online asset planning methodology to fulfill the sensible achievability of MCC. They embrace asset reservation to lessen the additional vitality utilization brought about by multi-offloading.

The work [53] is an adaptable assistance provisioning technique dependent on setting requirements for improving client involvement with administration situated on the portable cloud. The proposed enhancement issue decays into two. The parameters (application and datacenter providers) undergo interplay by using ideal value factors. It uses setting attention to assort and versatile parameters of a flexible cloud. This method influences user fulfillment. The versatile cloud framework settings include the portable application inclinations, the different devices' profile, and the data.

Cost Efficiency

The cloud cost depends on the membership model. It tends to pay more only as prices arise. The cloud limits cost of different administrations.

Yang *et al.*, 2014 [54] recommended a novel method dependent on compiler code examination. The procedure adequately decreases the moved information size by moving just the fundamental load objects, and the stack outlines referenced in the server.

Chunlin & Layuan, (2015) [55] suggested the expense and vitality aware provisioning plan for portable customers in the versatile cloud. The method incorporates a two-fold improvement process. In the primary stage enhancement process, the dynamic cloud client gives the one of a kind ideal installment to the cloud supplier under the expense and vitality imperative and enhances its advantage. In the second-organize streamlining process, a versatile cloud supplier runs numerous VMs to execute the employments for portable cloud clients. The cloud suppliers likewise need to amplify the income. The proposed administration provisioning calculation is associated with the cloud datacenter supplier's advancement and versatile cloud client's enhancement, which are directed by two schedules.

The recommendation [56] is a new green arrangement that spares cell phone vitality and simultaneously accomplishes the green ICT goal. The MCC moves the substance from the preliminary cloud server to the neighborhood cloud server transitory. The Internet Service Provider (ISP) gives the MCC, which holds the requirement for the cell phone organization. Kim *et al.*, (2015) [57] recommend control calculations for the versatile clients and cloud service provider (CSP). It uses two unique situations. In a non-collaboration scenario, an NC-UC calculation for the portable clients and an NC-CC calculation for the CSP to limit each cost for given defer imperatives. In the participation situation, the creators propose a CP-JC computation for both cloud clients and CSP to restrict the total expenses of them for the given defer limitations.

Mobility and Availability

Cloud gives benefits that are accessible to any place the end client. It bolsters simple access to data and obliges the requirements of clients in various time zones and geographic areas.

Guerrero-Contreras *et al.*, (2016) [58] suggested a proposition that depends on an assistance replication scheme. The design gets along with a self-design approach for the enactment/hibernation of the reproductions of the administration relies upon applicable setting data from the portable framework. The work presents an environment for programming engineering. The method aims to give a versatile and energy-efficient answer for the accessibility of administrations in transferable clouds. The all-encompassing variants of the conventional Minimum Execution Time heuristic and the Minimum Completion Time heuristic, and a portability forecast based offloading heuristic [59] is a suggestion to tackle the versatility issue in cell phone clouds. MET (Minimum Execution Time) and MCT (Minimum Completion Time) heuristics stretch out to take care of the portability issue in versatile distributed computing.

The multi-criteria decision making TOPSIS technique [60] organizes the administration giving assets, for example, Cloud, Cloudlet, and companion cell phones. The unrivaled pick the offloading. While benefiting administration from an asset, the proposed vertical handoff calculation triggers handoff from an asset to another. It occurs when the vitality utilization of the gadget increments or the association time with the asset diminishes. Also, the parallel execution performs to moderate the vitality of the cell phone. The aftereffects of exploratory arrangement with opennebula Cloud stage, Cloudlets and Android cell phones on different system conditions, recommend that handoff starting with one asset then onto the next is by a long shot progressively useful as far as vitality utilization, and administration accessibility for portable clients is concerned.

Backup and Disaster Recovery

Facilitation of the cloud disentangles supports and recuperating information. The information presently lives on the cloud, not on a physical gadget itself. The cloud itself is utilized exclusively now and again as a reinforcement archive of the information put away in neighborhood PCs. Cloud storage administration utilization encourages auxiliary reinforcement and fiasco of information recuperation without the requirement for particular reinforcement servers at the optional area or distributed storage administration. Reinforcement information streams (RIS) moves to a distributed storage administration. The RIS, reinforcement metadata is created for every RIS. The reinforcement metadata [61] is adjusted to design a reinforcement server to recover and get to the information in the RIS. The recuperation reinforcement framework is associated with the distributed storage administration to obtain information. The recuperation reinforcement framework refreshes with the reinforcement metadata. It arranges the recuperation reinforcement framework to recover and get to the information in the reinforcement information stream RIS.

Jian-Hua & Nan (2011) [62] portrays the design of distributed storage and presents the arrangement of the catastrophe recuperation and different applications in between private distributed storage. This method can accomplish genuinely distributed computing. The best element of this framework is to utilize the Storage Area Network (SAN) to help the application information get to backup. Users use the information to get to the administration of the distributed storage framework. Between private distributed storage with the given clients, a worth includes stockpiling administrations.

A spreading over capacity interface encourages the utilization of distributed storage benefits by capacity customers and may perform information reduplication. The spread over capacity interface may incorporate nearby stockpiling for reserving information from capacity customers. A fiasco recuperation application [63] is the first and second crossing stockpiling interfaces. The second traversing stockpiling interface accommodates at any rate debacle recuperation tasks. The second traversing stockpiling interface incorporates neighborhood stockpiling to improve information extraction. A duplicate of the neighborhood reserve of the first spreading over the capacity interface is moved to the second nearby amass while the primary system area is working. In the case of a fiasco influencing the preliminary system area, the second crossing stockpiling interface can give information access to the principal arrange area's information with improved execution from utilizing the duplicate of neighborhood reserve in the second nearby stockpiling.

A solicitation to get help related to a reinforcement application employs versatile media transmission arrange from a customer running on the portable media transmission gadget [64]. The reinforcement application transmission within the interest of the customer running on the versatile media transmission gadget to furnish access to the administration related to a reinforcement application.

The work is a test application running on the first stage of prior server design usage for catastrophe recuperation [65]. A first solicitation sent to the test application includes verifying the primary petition by a first test application. A subsequent solicitation is sent to the test application to create test information. A third solicitation is sent to a second stage in the next server to switch traffic for the test application from the principal occurrence to a subsequent occasion running in the succeeding server. A fourth solicitation sent to the test application includes verifying that the fourth solicitation for constant happening. A fifth solicitation is sent to the test application to approve information duplicated from the principal server to the subsequent server. Assurance made concerns about whether fiasco recuperation is successful.

Resiliency and Redundancy

The distributed computing foundation is a well-founded design by adding strength provided by various resources. The cloud gives programmed failover between equipment frameworks out of the container. The debacle reinforcement recuperation administrations are additionally regularly included.

PlanetCloud [66] includes a reliable fine-grained virtualization layer. PlanetCloud utilizes the ideas of use virtualization, and fractionation uses naturally flexible and miniaturized scale virtual machines. Such work detaches the running application from the preliminary physical asset empowering consistent execution over different assets. It lightens the burden movement and minimal effort of disappointment. Fundamental to PlanetCloud is an asset gauging and determination system, which furnishes a MAC with future suitable asset accessibility in existence.

Zhao & Dán (2017) [67] addressed this issue by thinking about Virtual Process

Control Functions (VPF). The arrangement costs are acquired by holding MEC assets, executing VPF occasions, and by information transmission. The proposal of VPF situation calculation is dependent on summed up Bender's deterioration and direct unwinding of the subsequent sub-issues. This measure adequately decreases the number of whole number factors to that of the quantity of MEC hubs.

The suggestion [68] is the biologically-inspired resilient autonomic cloud (BioRac). It utilizes organically propelled strategies and staggered tunable excess methods to build assault and misuse flexibility in cloud computing. The cloud administration mapping into organic-like structures alludes to creatures. For each help creature, they have expanded on-request a group of cells that approach all the necessary physical and consistent assets to run the capacities related to the life form cells.

Pacheco *et al.*, (2016) [69] have recommended a stage that offers secure and good administrations for Enhanced Living Environment (ELE). The fundamental segments are the ELE end hubs, a secure entryway, and a protected and robust distributed computing framework. End hubs gather ELE factors and human indications that are put away safely in the cloud utilizing a protected entryway. The protected entryway oversees correspondence between the end hubs, and the cloud administrations use biocyber measurements for validation. The cloud design gives the required ELE administrations whenever and from anyplace in a versatile way.

Scalability and Performance

Adaptability work considers the attributes of cloud arrangements. The cloud occasions are sent naturally on request, and therefore, clients are paid uniquely for the necessary applications and information stockpiling. The cloud is scaled to meet the necessities modification in the IT framework requests. As far as execution, the cloud uses dispersed framework structures that offer phenomenal calculation speed.

The proposal [70] is a Cloudlet-based MCC framework targeting decreasing the power utilization and the system deferral of sight and sound applications while utilizing MCC. The MCC ideas with the proposed Cloudlet structure incorporation with another versatile system for the MCC model.

MAPCloud [71] is a hybrid, layered cloud engineering comprising of the neighborhood and open cloud. It shows how it tends to use to increment both the execution and versatility of portable applications. The work process undertakings and expect to ideally disintegrate the arrangement of errands to execute on the versatile customer and 2-level cloud design. The design considers various QoS factors, for example, power, cost, and deferral.

Tysowski & Hasan (2013) [72] suggested a convention acknowledgment on financially versatile and cloud stages. The system exhibits genuine benchmarks that show the viability of the plan. Any client may scramble for information utilizing the general parcel key put away in the cloud. In any case, the cloud supplier cannot unscramble any client information put away on its premises as it cannot get to the secret proprietor's information. The encryptor of a message may confine its qualified readership by choosing a necessary arrangement of traits.

FollowMe Cloud (FMC) [73] is an innovation created at NEC Laboratories Europe. The system permits straightforward movement of administrations in TCP/IP systems, on account of the dynamic arrangement of facilitated OpenFlow switches situated at the edge of the system. FMC engineering depends on participating FMC controllers in the systems. FMC controllers alter parcel sending, and administrations are straightforwardly overseen by the system foundation, with no need to reconfigure the end frameworks.

Quick Deployment and Ease Integration

A cloud can be conveyed and run in a brief period. On a similar angle, presenting another client in the cloud happens promptly and rapidly by wiping out. It keeps up periods. As the cloud applications incorporation happens consequently in the cloud establishments, client and business upholding to pick the necessary administrations and applications that best suit their inclinations, while spending the least exertion in incorporating and tweaking those applications.

Verbelen *et al*, (2013) [74] is structured and assessed diagram. It divides calculations that distribute programming segments to machines in the cloud while limiting the required transfer speed. The creator's present calculations to segment a product application, made out of various categories. The segmentation depends on different interconnected machines in the cloud with differing limits while limiting the correspondence cost between the parts. A staggered KL based calculation display as a quick partitioner who permits real-time arrangement estimations.

The design [75] is a Wearable 2.0 social insurance framework to improve QoE and QoS of the cutting edge medicinal services framework. In the proposed framework sensors, anodes, and wires, are the primary segments are gathered to analyze clients' physiological condition. They get the examination aftereffects of clients' wellbeing and enthusiastic status using cloud-based machine knowledge.

The recommendation [76] is a novel structure to process the tactile information gathered by the sensors. They empower the transmissions of noticeable information to versatile clients in a quick, dependable, and secure way. The information traffic observing, sifting, expectation, pressure, and decompression capacities undergo fusion in the sensor portal and the cloud passage. Information encryption and decoding procedures are applied in the cloud, cell phones, and sensor and cloud passages to improve limits.

Environment-Friendly

The cloud spares vitality because it takes fewer assets to register to contrast in the average IT framework irrespective of the fundamental and required assets that are devoured by the structure.

The suggestion [77] is a robust vitality cloudlet-based portable distributed computing model concentrating on unraveling the extra vitality utilization during the remote interchanges in dynamic cloudlets - based model. The primary commitments of the work are twofold. Initially, the proposal is the principal investigator tackling vitality squander issues inside the administration condition. Second, the proposed model furnishes future research with a rule and hypothetical backings.

MobSched [78] is a flexible activity scheduler and a versatile neighborly MapReduce system. The two strategies empower engineers to utilize the MapReduce programming model with regards to MANET. MobSched, which depends on a straight programming definition, can effectively enhance different goals. For example, it can remain in control or potentially throughput while being compelled with prerequisites.

APPLICATIONS AND USE CASES

The sensor-cloud aims to provisioning the sensed reading to the client device anytime, anywhere. It also imparts portability to its clients. The facility adds advantages to the cloud. The portable Sensor-cloud system usage in many applications is the discussion of the section. Table **1** lists the application usage of MCC.

Garcia & Kalva (2011) [79] examine a utilization situation where PC clouds make use in the transcoding of media substance. They focus on their favorable circumstances in a minimal effort, for example, HTTP Live. Hadoop-map/Reduce is the product system for composing applications that form a lot of information in parallel to large groups of item equipment in a dependable manner. It executes the Map/lessen model in free dissemination, for example, Apache Hadoop, hurray Hadoop and Cloudera.

Ku & Gerla (2014) [80] suggested a methodology for Software-Defined Networking (SDN) based Mobile Cloud designs, concentrating on Ad hoc systems. The necessary center parts to construct an SDN-based Mobile Cloud include varieties of resources required to oblige to diverse remote situations. Examples include portability and questionable remote connection conditions.

Table 1. Applications of MCC.

Applications	Usage
Mobile commerce	Finance, Advertising, shopping
Mobile learning	electronic learning (e-learning)
Mobile healthcare	Comprehensive health monitoring, Intelligent emergency management system, Health-aware mobile devices, Pervasive access to healthcare information, Pervasive lifestyle incentive management
Mobile gaming	M-games
Others	Keyword-based searching, Voice-based searching, Tag-based searching

Vartiainen & Väänänen-Vainio-Mattila (2010) [81] presented the Image Exchange model. The design is a photograph sharing Internet administration that plans from the distributed computing point of view. The creators have assessed Image Exchange through two clients examines and portray significant ramifications for distributed computing on cell phones.

CHALLENGES

Every system on its own has a set of advantages and disadvantages. Consider Mobile Sensor-cloud. It provides seamless access to the system by supporting multiple clients and availing portability. But these devices do encounter many challenges. This section explains some of the opposition in MCC.

Heterogeneity

MCC means to increase a large number of cell phones utilizing heterogeneous space of cloud through different remote technologies. Intra-framework handover is a less testing undertaking because of the internal homogeneity of drawing in advance. The tending to between framework handover is progressively muddled because of signal transmission challenges between different conditions. To handle numerous difficulties, the idea of consistent availability among various remote innovations assumes a crucial job. It requires solid intra-framework and intersystem handoff plans. To acknowledge the compatible availability of crosswise (heterogeneous remote systems) prospering idea of cutting edge remote systems with the thought of all IP-based frameworks is focused. The authors have suggested various models addressing heterogeneity.

The horizontal heterogeneity in the MCC area utilizing a subjective approach and investigate primary prerequisites approaches toward perfect MCC. The system provides three preliminary gatherings of pervasiveness, trust, and vitality proficiency. The tripod [82] would be a scale to assess the convenience of cloud administrations, versatile cloud arrangements, and approaches.

The proposition [83] comprises three significant layers, to be specific Service Oriented Architecture (SOA), mediator, and foundation. The fundamental quality of this design is in its multi-level foundation layer that uses frameworks from three primary wellsprings of Clouds. Over the framework layer, the referee layer focuses on ordering Services and allot the reasonable assets to them, dependent on a few measurements, for example, asset necessity, dormancy, and security.

The creators have proposed [84] a leveled distributed computing engineering to upgrade execution by including a different unique cloud framework. The technology is adaptable by incredible cell phones to a conventional general static cloud. The unusual cloud works on the various remote design where gadget-t--gadget correspondence usage for information transmission between client gadgets. The principle preferred position of the proposal is an expansion in the general limit of a portable system. The limit can be suggested through improved channel usage and traffic offloading.

The creators suggested [85] a drone-cell management framework (DMF) profiting the collaboration among software-defined networking (SDN), Network function virtualization (NFV), and distributed computing. The automation cells carry the stock to where the request is and sets new outskirts for the heterogeneity in 5G systems. The proposed model [86] is called Energy-Aware Heterogeneous Cloud Management (EA-HCM) model, and the preliminary calculation is the Heterogeneous Task Assignment Algorithm (HTA2). The emphasis is on the vitality sparing issue. It considers the vital squander when undertakings are allowed to remote cloud servers or heterogeneous center processors.

Quality of Service

QoS alludes to a lot of properties includes targeted and client experience assessment problems. The targets include transmission rate, defer fluctuation, parcel misfortune, cost, and notoriety. Some of the client-related issues include client experience, trust, protection concern, and fulfillment degree. The numerous particular components influence the transferable cloud administration. The domain incorporates equipment and programming impediments of cell phones, the signal quality of versatile systems, versatility of portable clients, and so forth. Along these lines, giving QoS affirmation to portable cloud administrations requires a further developed framework and more successful systems than customary cloud administrations.

The creators [87] have defined data transfer capacity redistribution as a utility augmentation issue. They have unraveled it utilizing an altered plummeting offer closeout. In the proposed plan, named Auction based bandwidth redistribution (AQUM), every door totals the requests of all the interfaces versatile hubs and provides offers the necessary measure of data transmission.

Mobile Social Cloud Computing (MSCC) is a figuring situation that incorporates informal organization based distributed computing and cell phones. In the registering condition, a portable client can become an individual from a casual community through genuine connections. The creators [88] have utilized Content Addressable Network (CAN) as the hidden MSCC has to deal with the areas of cell phones. Adaptation to internal failure and QoS planning comprises four sub-booking calculations -malignant client sifting, cloud administration conveyance, QoS provisioning, and replication and burden adjusting.

The authors propose a novel structure [89] demonstrating versatile applications as location-time workflows (LTW) of assignments. The work insists on client portability designs to be versatile assistance use designs. The proposition is a productive heuristic calculation. It considers Mobility-aware optimal service allocation in mobile cloud computing (MuSIC) that can perform well by indicating 78% of ideal and 30% superior to basic strategies. It additionally scales well to countless clients while guaranteeing high application QoS.

The plan is an edge-based approach [90] to improve the QoS of MCC by the participation of the nearby cloud and Internet cloud assets, which takes the benefits of low inactivity of the neighborhood cloud and copious computational of assets of the Internet cloud all the while. This arrangement additionally applies a need line as far as deferring necessities of utilization.

The work [91] defined an advancement issue for dynamic asset sharing of portable clients in a versatile distributed computing hotspot with a cloudlet as a semi-Markov decision process (SMDP). SMDP changes into a linear programming (LP) model and fathoms to acquire an ideal arrangement.

A QoS based board model dependent on Fuzzy Cognitive Map (FCM) is proposed [92]. The proposal is a novel cross-arrangement for Hybrid Mobile Computing (HMC) systems. The system is QoS-aware, and it boosts the inhabitant's income while fulfilling the QoS necessities.

Security and Privacy

The versatile distributed computing offering in either cell phone condition or portable installed framework condition. Versatile processing is incorporating with distributed computing on account of the primitive qualities of the cloud model. Some of the examples include on-request self-administration, system get to, asset pooling, fast flexibility, and estimated administrations. Additionally, distributed computing is being well known to versatile clients as it can give cloud-like administrations. In [93], the creators show that at any rate, six attributes are fundamental for MCC. To add security to the system, the authors have provided various suggestions.

The proposal [94] outlines the general idea of a new application model. It breaks down its remarkable security prerequisites and presents plan contemplations to fabricate secure flexible applications. As initial steps, the creators propose an answer for verification and the secure session between websites running gadgets and those on the cloud. The proposal secures movement by approving cloud websites to get to delicate client information, for example, employing outer web administrations.

Zheng, 1996 [95] suggests another validation and key dissemination convention. It uses a communication diversion in a portable system. An especially intriguing element of the new proposition permits the validation of a base station by a versatile client.

The recommendation [96] is an interruption recognition framework utilizing a few parameters. For example, the CPU burden and the circle get to assess the power utilization, using a straight relapse model, enabling us to discover the vitality utilized on every procedure premise.

Sacramento *et al.*, (2005) [97] depict the plan and usage of a protection administration called Context Privacy Service (CoPS). This kind of service usage controls how, when, and to whom to reveal a client's data. The analysis is the consequences of an end-client overview and experience detailed by other research gatherings. CoPS are discretionary assistance setting that provision middleware Module Cloud Offloading (MoCA). It permits clients of setting and is area aware applications to characterize and deal with their protection arrangements in regards to the revelation of their setting data. The principle highlights upheld by CoPS are bunch based access control, critical and various leveled protection rules, blended activity connection, and rule explicitness investigation. Bilogrevic *et al.*, (2011) [98] suggested two security safeguarding calculations for the fair rendezvous point (FRVP) issue and diagnostically assessment. The protection is uninvolved and dynamic in antagonistic situations.

FUTURE DIRECTIONS

Distributed computing is the conveyance of registering as assistance instead of an item, whereby shared assets, programming, and data provision to PCs and different gadgets as a utility over a system. It gives calculation, programming, and capacity benefits that do not require end-client information on the physical area and framework design. Distributed computing research oversees the processing, stockpiling, and correspondence assets shared by various clients in a virtualized and separated condition. Sensor-cloud aims to provide reading to the clients on their request. The clients will be able to view the interpretation in an unsupervised environment. MCC attempts to engage the portable client by giving universal and useful techniques, payinsg little attention to the asset impediments of cell phones. The immediate income of the dynamic cloud market will develop to about $68 billion by 2017. The merge of these technologies has provided a lot of advantages to reducing human effort. But the area also raises some concern which needs working in the future. The following are some of the considerations in MCC.

- Due to the restricted assets and abilities of compact gadgets and sensors in MCC environments, future research in planning security conventions and calculations. It should concentrate more on control proficiency and deferral of such security calculations and how to parcel them on cloud and cell phones.

- User versatility includes an expanded degree of multifaceted nature from the security point. The security level of portable clients can change from area to area now and again and quickly. Availability conditions in various locations likewise include unpredictability.

- The utilization of security administrations for versatile clients in an MCC domain like Location-based Service (LBS) will build the intricacy of inquiry handling.

The work [49] needs to stretch out. The model has to think about increasingly complex application situations. Some instances include assortment out of assignments with timing requirements that keep up priority connections and the utilization of other framework resources. The other course is going further into the net defer forecast issue since this is the primary angle in planning choices that consider the remote assets in an MCC setting.

The creators [66] are building up a security instrument to safeguard the protection, security requirements of MAC/HMAC asset suppliers while enabling numerous clients to share self-governing assets.

REFERENCES

[1]   H. Liang, D. Huang, L.X. Cai, X. Shen, and D. Peng, "Resource allocation for security services in mobile cloud computing", *IEEE Conference on Computer Communications Workshops (INFOCOM WKSHPS)*, 2011, pp. 191-195 Shanghai, China.
        [http://dx.doi.org/10.1109/INFCOMW.2011.5928806]

[2]   K. Kumar, J. Liu, Y.H. Lu, and B. Bhargava, "A survey of computation offloading for mobile systems", *Mob. Netw. Appl.,* vol. 18, no. 1, pp. 129-140, 2013.
        [http://dx.doi.org/10.1007/s11036-012-0368-0]

[3]   X. Chen, "Decentralized computation offloading game for mobile cloud computing", *IEEE Trans. Parallel Distrib. Syst.,* vol. 26, no. 4, pp. 974-983, 2014.
        [http://dx.doi.org/10.1109/TPDS.2014.2316834]

[4]   L.F. Pau, "Differential games and a Nash equilibrium searching algorithm", *SIAM J. Control,* vol. 13, no. 4, pp. 835-852, 1975.
        [http://dx.doi.org/10.1137/0313050]

[5]   X. Chen, L. Jiao, W. Li, and X. Fu, "Efficient multi-user computation offloading for mobile-edge cloud computing", *IEEE/ACM Trans. Netw.,* vol. 24, no. 5, pp. 2795-2808, 2015.
        [http://dx.doi.org/10.1109/TNET.2015.2487344]

[6]   R.B. Myerson, "Refinements of the Nash equilibrium concept", *Int. J. Game Theory,* vol. 7, no. 2, pp. 73-80, 1978.
        [http://dx.doi.org/10.1007/BF01753236]

[7]   D. Huang, P. Wang, and D. Niyato, "A dynamic offloading algorithm for mobile computing", *IEEE Trans. Wirel. Commun.,* vol. 11, no. 6, pp. 1991-1995, 2012.
        [http://dx.doi.org/10.1109/TWC.2012.041912.110912]

[8]   C-C. Chu, and H-C. Tsai, "Application of Lyapunov-based adaptive neural network UPFC damping controllers for transient stability enhancement", In: *IEEE Power and Energy Society General Meeting-Conversion and Delivery of Electrical Energy in the 21ˢᵗ Century*, Pittsburgh, PA, USA, 2008, pp. 1-6.

[9]   S. Deng, L. Huang, J. Taheri, and A.Y. Zomaya, "Computation offloading for service workflow in mobile cloud computing", *IEEE Trans. Parallel Distrib. Syst.,* vol. 26, no. 12, pp. 3317-3329, 2014.
        [http://dx.doi.org/10.1109/TPDS.2014.2381640]

[10]   M. Gen, R. Cheng, and L. Lin, Network models and optimization: Multiobjective genetic algorithm approach., 3rd ed., Mitsuo Gen, Runwei Cheng, and Lin Lin, Eds. London, UK: Springer Science & Business Media., 2008,

[11]   D. Kovachev, T. Yu, and R. Klamma, "Adaptive computation offloading from mobile devices into the

cloud", In: *IEEE 10th International Symposium on Parallel and Distributed Processing with Applications*, Leganes, Spain, 2012, pp. 784-791.
[http://dx.doi.org/10.1109/ISPA.2012.115]

[12]   M. Mamei, and F. Zambonelli, "Programming pervasive and mobile computing applications with the TOTA middleware", *Second IEEE Annual Conference on Pervasive Computing and Communications*, 2004, pp. 263-273 Orlando, FL, USA.
[http://dx.doi.org/10.1109/PERCOM.2004.1276864]

[13]   P.J. McCann, and G.C. Roman, *"Compositional programming abstractions for mobile computing"*, *IEEE Transactions on Software Engineering*, vol. 24, no. 2, pp. 97-110, Febraury 1998.
[http://dx.doi.org/10.1109/32.666824]

[14]   N. Fernando, S.W. Loke, and W. Rahayu, "Honeybee: A programming framework for mobile crowd computing", *International Conference on Mobile and Ubiquitous Systems: Computing, Networking, and Services*, 2012, pp. 224-236 Beijing, China.

[15]   G. Welling, and B.R. Badrinath, "Mobjects: Programming support for environment directed application policies in mobile computing", In: *ECOOP'95 Workshop on Mobility and Replication*, vol. 28, Tokyo, Japan, 1995, pp. 1-4.

[16]   C.F. Lai, H.C. Chao, Y.X. Lai, and J. Wan, "Cloud-assisted real-time transrating for http live streaming", *IEEE Wirel. Commun.*, vol. 20, no. 3, pp. 62-70, 2013.
[http://dx.doi.org/10.1109/MWC.2013.6549284]

[17]   S.M. Saranya, and M. Vijayalakshmi, "Interactive mobile live video learning system in cloud environment", *International Conference on Recent Trends in Information Technology (ICRTIT)*, 2011, pp. 673-677 Chennai, Tamil Nadu, India.
[http://dx.doi.org/10.1109/ICRTIT.2011.5972458]

[18]   G. Xi, and X. Zhang, "On adaptive live streaming in mobile cloud computing environments with D2D cooperation", *in 21st International Conference on Telecommunications (ICT), Lisbon, Portugal*, pp. 405-409, 2014.

[19]   M. Garcia-Pineda, S. Felici-Castell, and J. Segura-Garcia, "Using factor analysis techniques to find out objective video quality metrics for live video streaming over cloud mobile media services", *Network Protocols and Algorithms*, vol. 8, no. 1, pp. 126-147, 2016.
[http://dx.doi.org/10.5296/npa.v8i1.8850]

[20]   F. Chen, C. Zhang, F. Wang, and J. Liu, "Crowdsourced live streaming over the cloud", *IEEE Conference on Computer Communications (INFOCOM)*, 2015, pp. 2524-2532 Kowloon, Hong Kong.
[http://dx.doi.org/10.1109/INFOCOM.2015.7218642]

[21]   M. R. Landis, A. J. Yeates, and T. J. Gavin, "Method for managing data transfer between computing devices", *Software 5, 588, 148*, December 24, 1996.

[22]   E. Todeschini, R. M. Hussey, and P. Crimm, "Mobile computing device with data cognition software", *14/462,801,*, 2016.

[23]   K. B. Jackson Jr, "Methods, systems and computer program products for transferring files from a data processing server to a remote/mobile data processing node", *Software 5, 819, 274*, October 6, 1998.

[24]   G. Kimchi, R. Barga, V. Gupta, Z. Apter, and S. Paparizos, "Computing system for managing data", *Software 9, 172, 708*, October 27, 2015.

[25]   I. Mehmood, M. Sajjad, and S.W. Baik, "Video summarization based tele-endoscopy: a service to efficiently manage visual data generated during wireless capsule endoscopy procedure", *J. Med. Syst.*, vol. 38, no. 9, p. 109, 2014.
[http://dx.doi.org/10.1007/s10916-014-0109-y] [PMID: 25037715]

[26]   B. Welingkar, and J. Nair, "Restoring of data to mobile computing device", *Software 8, 583, 602*, November 12, 2013.

[27]   W. E. Sobel, and B. Hernacki, "Methods and systems for securely managing multimedia data captured by mobile computing devices", *Software 8, 433, 895,* April 30, 2013.

[28]   M.R. Rahimi, J. Ren, C.H. Liu, A.V. Vasilakos, and N. Venkatasubramanian, "Mobile cloud computing: A survey, state of art and future directions", *Mob. Netw. Appl.,* vol. 19, no. 2, pp. 133-143, 2014.
[http://dx.doi.org/10.1007/s11036-013-0477-4]

[29]   D. Huang, X. Zhang, M. Kang, and J. Luo, "MobiCloud: building secure cloud framework for mobile computing and communication", In: *5th IEEE international symposium on service oriented system engineering,* Nanjing, China, 2010, pp. 27-34.
[http://dx.doi.org/10.1109/SOSE.2010.20]

[30]   G. Rayner, "Protective encasement for mobile computing device", *Software 9, 300, 344,* March 29, 2016.

[31]   I. B. Peev, S. R. Shell, K. J. Savage, H. M. Dang, and N. M. Hofmeister, "Installing software on a mobile computing device using the rollback and security features of a configuration manager", *Software 6,993,760,* January 31, 2006.

[32]   M. Spreitzer, and M. Theimer, "Scalable, secure mobile computing with location information", *Commun. ACM,* vol. 36, no. 7, pp. 27-28, 1993.
[http://dx.doi.org/10.1145/159544.159558]

[33]   A. Inoue, "Mobile computer and method of packet encryption and authentication in mobile computing based on security policy of visited network", *Software 6, 170, 057,* January 2, 2001.

[34]   K. Xi, T. Ahmad, F. Han, and J. Hu, "A fingerprint based bio-cryptographic security protocol designed for client/server authentication in mobile computing environment", *Secur. Commun. Netw.,* vol. 4, no. 5, pp. 487-499, 2011.
[http://dx.doi.org/10.1002/sec.225]

[35]   J. Oberheide, K. Veeraraghavan, E. Cooke, J. Flinn, and F. Jahanian, "Virtualized in-cloud security services for mobile devices", *first workshop on virtualization in mobile computing,* 2008, pp. 31-35 Breckenridge, Colorado.
[http://dx.doi.org/10.1145/1622103.1629656]

[36]   N. Mallikharjuna Rao, C. Sasidhar, and V. Sathyendra Kumar, "Cloud Computing Through Mobile-Learning", *Int. J. Adv. Comp. Sci. App. (IJACSA),* pp. 1-6, April 2012.

[37]   D. Huang, Z. Zhou, L. Xu, T. Xing, and Y. Zhong, "Secure data processing framework for mobile cloud computing", *IEEE Conference on Computer Communications Workshops (INFOCOM WKSHPS),* 2011, pp. 614-618 Shanghai, China.
[http://dx.doi.org/10.1109/INFCOMW.2011.5928886]

[38]   Z. Zhou, and D. Huang, "Efficient and secure data storage operations for mobile cloud computing", *In: 8th international conference on Network and service management (cnsm) and 2012 workshop on systems virtualiztion management (svm),* Las Vegas, NV, USA, pp. 37-45, 2012.

[39]   A. Klein, C. Mannweiler, J. Schneider, and H.D. Schotten, "Access schemes for mobile cloud computing", In: *11th International Conference on Mobile Data Management,* Kansas City, MO, USA, 2010, pp. 387-392.
[http://dx.doi.org/10.1109/MDM.2010.79]

[40]   W. Jia, H. Zhu, Z. Cao, L. Wei, and X. Lin, "SDSM: a secure data service mechanism in mobile cloud computing", *IEEE Conference on Computer Communications Workshops (INFOCOM WKSHPS),* 2011, pp. 1060-1065 Shanghai, China.
[http://dx.doi.org/10.1109/INFCOMW.2011.5928784]

[41]   R. Kaewpuang, D. Niyato, P. Wang, and E. Hossain, "A framework for cooperative resource management in mobile cloud computing", *IEEE J. Sel. Areas Comm.,* vol. 31, no. 12, pp. 2685-2700, 2013.

[http://dx.doi.org/10.1109/JSAC.2013.131209]

[42]   M. S. G. Sawant, and S. T. Singh, "A Survey on Strategy-Proof Pricing for Cloud Service Composition", *Imperial J. Interdis. Res.,* vol. 3, no. 1, 2017.

[43]   A.T. Lo'ai, R. Mehmood, E. Benkhlifa, and H. Song, "Mobile cloud computing model and big data analysis for healthcare applications", *IEEE Access,* vol. 4, pp. 6171-6180, 2016.
[http://dx.doi.org/10.1109/ACCESS.2016.2613278]

[44]   W.B. Lo'ai A Tawalbeh, and H. Song, "A Mobile Cloud Computing Model Using the Cloudlet Scheme for Big Data Applications", *First International Conference on Connected Health: Applications, Systems and Engineering Technologies (CHASE),* 2016, pp. 73-77 Washington, DC, USA.

[45]   A.T. Lo'ai, W. Bakhader, R. Mehmood, and H. Song, "Cloudlet-Based Mobile Cloud Computing for Healthcare Applications", *IEEE Global Communications Conference (GLOBECOM),* 2016, pp. 1-6 Washington, DC, USA.

[46]   W. Itani, A. Kayssi, and A. Chehab, "Energy-efficient incremental integrity for securing storage in mobile cloud computing", *International Conference on Energy Aware Computing,* 2010, pp. 37-45 Cairo, Egypt.
[http://dx.doi.org/10.1109/ICEAC.2010.5702296]

[47]   W. Ren, L. Yu, R. Gao, and F. Xiong, "Lightweight and compromise resilient storage outsourcing with distributed secure accessibility in mobile cloud computing", *Tsinghua Sci. Technol.,* vol. 16, no. 5, pp. 520-528, 2011.
[http://dx.doi.org/10.1016/S1007-0214(11)70070-0]

[48]   S. Barbarossa, S. Sardellitti, and P. Di Lorenzo, "Joint allocation of computation and communication resources in multiuser mobile cloud computing", In: *IEEE 14th workshop on signal processing advances in wireless communications (SPAWC),* Darmstadt, Germany, 2013, pp. 26-30.
[http://dx.doi.org/10.1109/SPAWC.2013.6612005]

[49]   H. Mora Mora, D. Gil, J. F. Colom López, and M. T. Signes Pont, "Flexible framework for real-time embedded systems based on mobile cloud computing paradigm", *Mobile information systems,* vol. 2015, pp. 1-4, Jun 2015.
[http://dx.doi.org/10.1155/2015/652462]

[50]   W. Ren, L. Zeng, R. Liu, and C. Cheng, *F2AC: a light-weight, fine-grained, and flexible access control scheme for file storage in mobile cloud computing.* Mobile Information Systems, 2016.

[51]   Z. Yan, X. Li, M. Wang, and A.V. Vasilakos, "Flexible data access control based on trust and reputation in cloud computing", *IEEE Trans. Cloud Comp.,* vol. 5, no. 3, pp. 485-498, 2015.

[52]   Z. Zhou, H. Zhang, L. Ye, and X. Du, "Cuckoo: flexible compute-intensive task offloading in mobile cloud computing", *Wirel. Commun. Mob. Comput.,* vol. 16, no. 18, pp. 3256-3268, 2016.
[http://dx.doi.org/10.1002/wcm.2757]

[53]   L. Chunlin, Y. Xin, and L. LaYuan, "Flexible service provisioning based on context constraint for enhancing user experience in service oriented mobile cloud", *J. Netw. Comput. Appl.,* vol. 66, pp. 250-261, 2016.
[http://dx.doi.org/10.1016/j.jnca.2016.03.003]

[54]   S. Yang, "Techniques to minimize state transfer costs for dynamic execution offloading in mobile cloud computing", *IEEE Trans. Mobile Comput.,* vol. 13, no. 11, pp. 2648-2660, 2014.
[http://dx.doi.org/10.1109/TMC.2014.2307293]

[55]   L. Chunlin, and L. Layuan, "Cost and energy aware service provisioning for mobile client in cloud computing environment", *J. Supercomput.,* vol. 71, no. 4, pp. 1196-1223, 2015.
[http://dx.doi.org/10.1007/s11227-014-1345-0]

[56]   M. Altamimi, and K. Naik, "The concept of a mobile cloud computing to reduce energy cost of smartphones and ICT systems", *International Conference on Information and Communication on*

Technology, 2011, pp. 79-86 Kyoto, Japan.
[http://dx.doi.org/10.1007/978-3-642-23447-7_8]

[57]   Y. Kim, J. Kwak, and S. Chong, "Dual-side dynamic controls for cost minimization in mobile cloud computing systems", *13ᵗʰ International Symposium on Modeling and Optimization in Mobile, Ad Hoc, and Wireless Networks (WiOpt),* 2015, pp. 443-450 Mumbai, India.
[http://dx.doi.org/10.1109/WIOPT.2015.7151104]

[58]   G. Guerrero-Contreras, J.L. Garrido, S. Balderas-Diaz, and C. Rodríguez-Domínguez, "A context-aware architecture supporting service availability in mobile cloud computing", *IEEE Trans. Serv. Comput.,* vol. 10, no. 6, pp. 956-968, 2016.
[http://dx.doi.org/10.1109/TSC.2016.2540629]

[59]   B. Li, Z. Liu, Y. Pei, and H. Wu, "Mobility prediction based opportunistic computational offloading for mobile device cloud", In: *IEEE 17ᵗʰ International Conference on Computational Science and Engineering,* Chengdu, China, 2014, pp. 786-792.
[http://dx.doi.org/10.1109/CSE.2014.161]

[60]   A. Ravi, and S.K. Peddoju, "Handoff strategy for improving energy efficiency and cloud service availability for mobile devices", *Wirel. Pers. Commun.,* vol. 81, no. 1, pp. 101-132, 2015.
[http://dx.doi.org/10.1007/s11277-014-2119-y]

[61]   N. Parab, "Cloud-based disaster recovery of backup data and metadata", *Software 9, 501, 365,* November 22, 2016.

[62]   Z. Jian-Hua, and Z. Nan, "Cloud computing-based data storage and disaster recovery", *2011 International Conference on Future Computer Science and Education,* 2011, pp. 629-632 Xi'an, China.
[http://dx.doi.org/10.1109/ICFCSE.2011.157]

[63]   G. Taleck, V. Keswani, N. Parab, and J. Mace, "Disaster recovery using local and cloud spanning deduplicated storage system", *Software 12/942, 988,* June 30, 2011.

[64]   T. Frencel, and S. Zajac, "Mobile access to backup and recovery services", *Software 8, 195, 153,* June 5, 2012.

[65]   S. Boshev, and M. Velev, "Automatic testing of disaster recovery scenarios in cloud environments", *Software 10, 275, 346,* April 30, 2019.

[66]   A. Khalifa, M. Azab, and M. Eltoweissy, "Resilient hybrid Mobile Ad-hoc Cloud over collaborating heterogeneous nodes", *10ᵗʰ IEEE International Conference on Collaborative Computing: Networking, Applications and Worksharing,* 2014, pp. 134-143 Miami, FL, USA.

[67]   P. Zhao, and G. Dán, Resilient placement of virtual process control functions in mobile edge clouds. IFIP Networking Conference (IFIP Networking) and Workshops. 2017.
[http://dx.doi.org/10.23919/IFIPNetworking.2017.8264849]

[68]   S. Hariri, M. Eltoweissy, and Y. Al-Nashif, "Biorac: biologically inspired resilient autonomic cloud", *Seventh Annual Workshop on Cyber Security and Information Intelligence Research,* 2011, p. 80 Oak Ridge, Tennessee, USA.

[69]   J. Pacheco, C. Tunc, P. Satam, and S. Hariri, "Secure and resilient cloud services for enhanced living environments", *IEEE Cloud Computing,* vol. 3, no. 6, pp. 44-52, 2016.
[http://dx.doi.org/10.1109/MCC.2016.129]

[70]   Y. Jararweh, F. Ababneh, A. Khreishah, and F. Dosari, "Scalable cloudlet-based mobile computing model", *9ᵗʰ International Conference on Future Networks and Communications (FNC'14),* 2014, pp. 434-441 Niagara Falls, Ontario, Canada.

[71]   M.R. Rahimi, N. Venkatasubramanian, S. Mehrotra, and A.V. Vasilakos, "MAPCloud: Mobile applications on an elastic and scalable 2-tier cloud architecture", In: *IEEE/ACM 5ᵗʰ international conference on utility and cloud computing,* Chicago, IL, USA, 2012, pp. 83-90.
[http://dx.doi.org/10.1109/UCC.2012.25]

[72]   P.K. Tysowski, and M.A. Hasan, "Hybrid attribute-and re-encryption-based key management for secure and scalable mobile applications in clouds", *IEEE Transactions on Cloud Computing,* vol. 1, no. 2, pp. 172-186, 2013.
[http://dx.doi.org/10.1109/TCC.2013.11]

[73]   R. Bifulco, M. Brunner, R. Canonico, P. Hasselmeyer, and F. Mir, "Scalability of a mobile cloud management system", In: *1st edition of the MCC workshop on Mobile cloud computing*, Helsinki, Finland, 2012, pp. 17-22.
[http://dx.doi.org/10.1145/2342509.2342514]

[74]   T. Verbelen, "T.l De Turck, F. Stevens, and B. Dhoedt, "Graph partitioning algorithms for optimizing software deployment in mobile cloud computing", *Future Gener. Comput. Syst.,* vol. 29, no. 2, pp. 451-459, 2013.
[http://dx.doi.org/10.1016/j.future.2012.07.003]

[75]   M. Chen, "Wearable 2.0: Enabling human-cloud integration in next generation healthcare systems", *IEEE Commun. Mag.,* vol. 55, no. 1, pp. 54-61, 2017.
[http://dx.doi.org/10.1109/MCOM.2017.1600410CM]

[76]   C. Zhu, "A novel sensory data processing framework to integrate sensor networks with mobile cloud", *IEEE Syst. J.,* vol. 10, no. 3, pp. 1125-1136, 2014.
[http://dx.doi.org/10.1109/JSYST.2014.2300535]

[77]   K. Gai, M. Qiu, H. Zhao, L. Tao, and Z. Zong, "Dynamic energy-aware cloudlet-based mobile cloud computing model for green computing", *J. Netw. Comput. Appl.,* vol. 59, pp. 46-54, 2016.
[http://dx.doi.org/10.1016/j.jnca.2015.05.016]

[78]   S. Sindia, "MobSched: Customizable scheduler for mobile cloud computing", *45th Southeastern symposium on system theory,* 2013, pp. 129-134 Waco, TX, USA.
[http://dx.doi.org/10.1109/SSST.2013.6524965]

[79]   A. Garcia, and H. Kalva, "Cloud transcoding for mobile video content delivery", *IEEE International Conference on Consumer Electronics (ICCE),* 2011, pp. 379-380 Las Vegas, NV, USA.
[http://dx.doi.org/10.1109/ICCE.2011.5722637]

[80]   I., Lu, Y. Ku, M. Gerla, "Software-defined mobile cloud: Architecture, services and use cases", In: *International wireless communications and mobile computing conference (IWCMC) ,* Nicosia, Cyprus, 2014, pp. 1-6.

[81]   E. Vartiainen, and K. Väänänen-Vainio-Mattila, "User experience of mobile photo sharing in the cloud", *9th International Conference on Mobile and Ubiquitous Multimedia,* 2010, p. 4 Limassol, Cyprus.
[http://dx.doi.org/10.1145/1899475.1899479]

[82]   Z. Sanaei, S. Abolfazli, A. Gani, and R.H. Khokhar, "Tripod of requirements in horizontal heterogeneous mobile cloud computing", *WSEAS International Conference on Computing, Information Systems and Communications,* 2012, pp. 1-6 Beijing, China.

[83]   Z. Sanaei, S. Abolfazli, A. Gani, and M. Shiraz, "SAMI: Service-based arbitrated multi-tier infrastructure for Mobile Cloud Computing", *1st IEEE International Conference on Communications in China Workshops (ICCC),* 2012, pp. 14-19 China.
[http://dx.doi.org/10.1109/ICCCW.2012.6316466]

[84]   M. Jo, T. Maksymyuk, B. Strykhalyuk, and C.H. Cho, "Device-to-device-based heterogeneous radio access network architecture for mobile cloud computing", *IEEE Wirel. Commun.,* vol. 22, no. 3, pp. 50-58, 2015.
[http://dx.doi.org/10.1109/MWC.2015.7143326]

[85]   I. Bor-Yaliniz, and H. Yanikomeroglu, "The new frontier in RAN heterogeneity: Multi-tier drone-cells", *IEEE Commun. Mag.,* vol. 54, no. 11, pp. 48-55, 2016.
[http://dx.doi.org/10.1109/MCOM.2016.1600178CM]

[86]   K. Gai, M. Qiu, and H. Zhao, "Energy-aware task assignment for mobile cyber-enabled applications in heterogeneous cloud computing", *J. Parallel Distrib. Comput.,* vol. 111, pp. 126-135, 2018.
[http://dx.doi.org/10.1016/j.jpdc.2017.08.001]

[87]   S. Misra, S. Das, M. Khatua, and M.S. Obaidat, "QoS-guaranteed bandwidth shifting and redistribution in mobile cloud environment", *IEEE Transactions on Cloud Computing,* vol. 2, no. 2, pp. 181-193, 2013.
[http://dx.doi.org/10.1109/TCC.2013.19]

[88]   S. Choi, K. Chung, and H. Yu, "Fault tolerance and QoS scheduling using CAN in mobile social cloud computing", *Cluster Comput.,* vol. 17, no. 3, pp. 911-926, 2014.
[http://dx.doi.org/10.1007/s10586-013-0286-3]

[89]   M.R. Rahimi, N. Venkatasubramanian, and A.V. Vasilakos, "MuSIC: Mobility-aware optimal service allocation in mobile cloud computing", *IEEE 6th International Conference on Cloud Computing,* 2013, pp. 75-82 Santa Clara, CA, USA.
[http://dx.doi.org/10.1109/CLOUD.2013.100]

[90]   T. Zhao, S. Zhou, X. Guo, Y. Zhao, and Z. Niu, A cooperative scheduling scheme of local cloud and internet cloud for delay-aware mobile cloud computing. *IEEE Globecom Workshops.* GC Wkshps: San Diego, CA, USA, 2015, pp. 1-6.
[http://dx.doi.org/10.1109/GLOCOMW.2015.7414063]

[91]   D.T. Hoang, D. Niyato, and P. Wang, "Optimal admission control policy for mobile cloud computing hotspot with cloudlet", *IEEE Wireless Communications and Networking Conference (WCNC),* 2012, pp. 3145-3149 Shanghai, China.
[http://dx.doi.org/10.1109/WCNC.2012.6214347]

[92]   P. Si, Q. Zhang, F.R. Yu, and Y. Zhang, "QoS-aware dynamic resource management in heterogeneous mobile cloud computing networks", *China Commun.,* vol. 11, no. 5, pp. 144-159, 2014.
[http://dx.doi.org/10.1109/CC.2014.6880470]

[93]   L. Zhong, B. Wang, and H. Wei, "Cloud computing applied in the mobile internet", *7th International conference on Computer Science & Education (ICCSE),* 2012, pp. 218-221 Melbourne, VIC, Australia.
[http://dx.doi.org/10.1109/ICCSE.2012.6295061]

[94]   X. Zhang, J. Schiffman, S. Gibbs, A. Kunjithapatham, and S. Jeong, Securing elastic applications on mobile devices for cloud computing. *Proceedings of the first ACM Cloud Computing Security Workshop,* CCSW 2009, Chicago, IL, USA, November 13, 2009.
[http://dx.doi.org/10.1145/1655008.1655026]

[95]   Y. Zheng, *An authentication and security protocol for mobile computing.* Mobile Communications, 1996, pp. 249-257.
[http://dx.doi.org/10.1007/978-0-387-34980-0_25]

[96]   D.C. Nash, T.L. Martin, D.S. Ha, and M.S. Hsiao, "Towards an intrusion detection system for battery exhaustion attacks on mobile computing devices", In: *3rd IEEE international conference on pervasive computing and communications workshops,* Kauai Island, HI, USA, 2005, pp. 141-145.
[http://dx.doi.org/10.1109/PERCOMW.2005.86]

[97]   V. Sacramento, M. Endler, and F.N. Nascimento, "A privacy service for context-aware mobile computing", *International Conference on Security and Privacy for Emerging Areas in Communications Networks (SECURECOMM'05),* 2005, pp. 182-193 Athens, Greece.
[http://dx.doi.org/10.1109/SECURECOMM.2005.8]

[98]   I. Bilogrevic, M. Jadliwala, K. Kalkan, J.P. Hubaux, and I. Aad, "Privacy in mobile computing for location-sharing-based services", *International Symposium on Privacy Enhancing Technologies Symposium,* 2011, pp. 77-96 Waterloo, ON, Canada.
[http://dx.doi.org/10.1007/978-3-642-22263-4_5]

CHAPTER 4

Fog Computing

Abstract: Fog processing is a dispersed computation worldview that goes about as a moderate layer in the middle of Cloud datacenters and IoT gadgets/sensors. It offers calculation, systems administration, and storerooms to Cloud-based administrations to stretch out nearer to the IoT gadgets/sensors. Since Cloud datacenters are geologically intensive, they frequently neglect to manage capacity and preparing requests of billions of geo-dispersed IoT gadgets/sensors. Accordingly, the clogged system experiences high inactivity in administration conveyance and low quality of Service (QoS). This chapter discusses the taxonomy, challenges, and future directions.

Keywords: Challenges, Fog computing, Future directions, Taxonomy.

INTRODUCTION

Fog processing proposal empowers the computation straightforwardly at the edge of the system. These systems can convey new applications and administrations for the eventual fate of the Internet. The switches can turn out to be new servers. In fog processing, offices or foundations that can give assets to administrations at the edge of the system are called fog devices.

The customary systems (administration parts) produce a Fog processing condition. Some examples include switches, switches, set-top boxes, intermediary servers, and Base Stations (BS). These parts are furnished with various processing, stockpiling, organizing, and so forth abilities. It can bolster administration application execution. Subsequently, the systems administration segments empower Fog registering to make enormous topographical dispersions of Cloud-based administrations. Fog processing encourages area awareness, versatility support, continuous cooperation, adaptability, and interoperability. In this manner, Fog processing can perform productively regarding service dormancy, control utilization, arranges traffic, capital and operational costs, content circulation, *etc*. In this way, Fog computation meets the prerequisites concerning IoT applications contrasted with an exclusive utilization of Cloud registering. Fig. (**1**) represents the layered architecture of fog computing.

Ambika Nagaraj

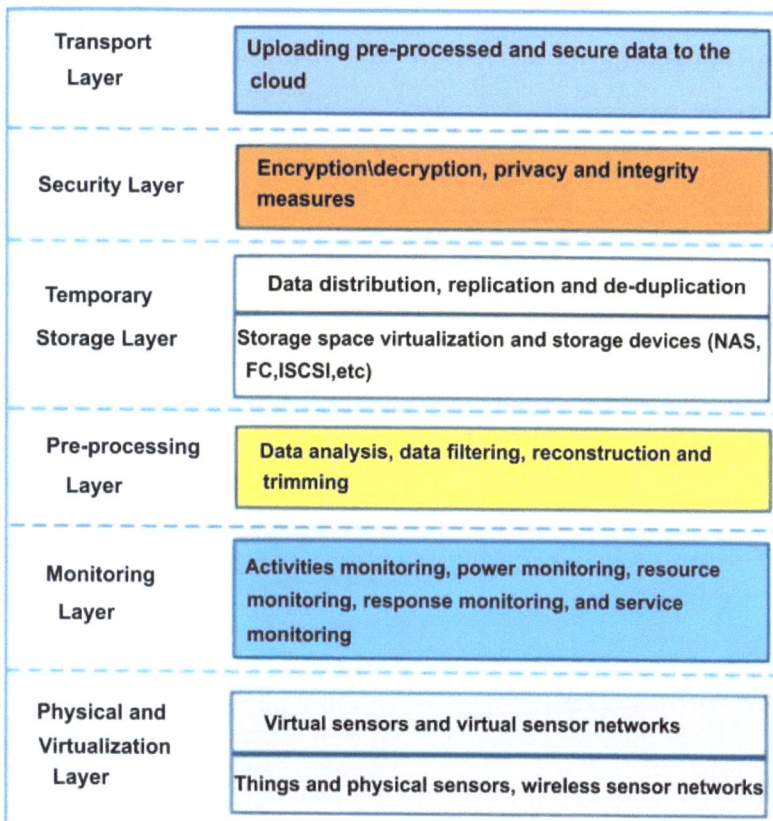

Fig. (1). Layered Architecture of Fog Computing [1].

TAXONOMY

Fog computing is composed of edge components that aid in better and efficient processing. The section provides different parts necessary to assemble into Fog. Fig. (2) explains the taxonomy of fog computing.

Fog Node Configuration

Fog computing is an intermediate component functioning between the cloud and end gadgets. This component brings preparing, stockpiling, and systems administration benefits nearer to the end gadgets themselves. These gadgets are called fog hubs. They can be conveyed anyplace with a system association. Any device with processing, stockpiling, and system availability can be a fog hub. Some examples of fog gateway include mechanical controllers, switches, inserted servers, and video reconnaissance cameras. The computational device with heterogeneous engineering and designs are fit to give foundation to Fog processing at the edge of the system. The section discusses various contributions.

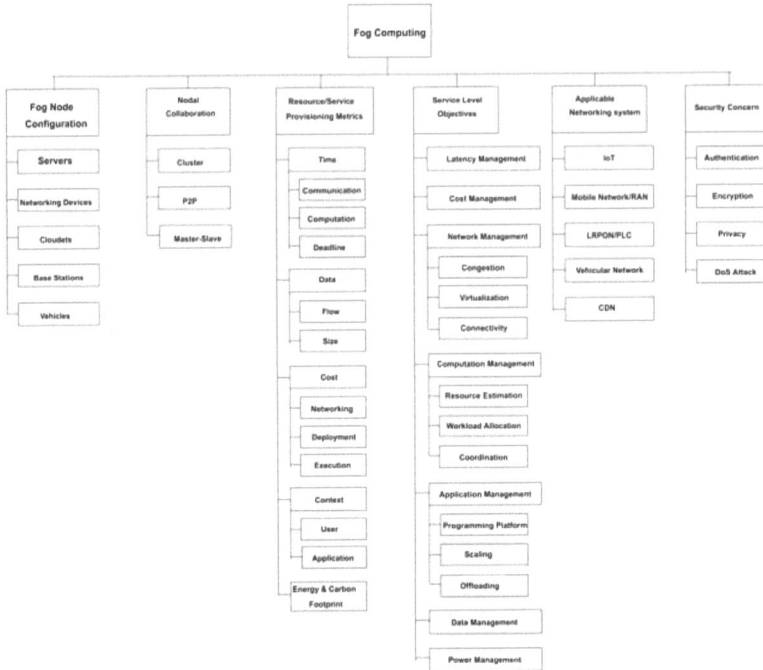

Fig. (2). Taxonomy of fog computing [2].

The proposal [3] initially works with the structure designed for IoT applications. It is dependent on inventive adaptability augmentations. The open-source is Kura and Docker-based containerization over testing and asset constrained fog hubs. The announced outcomes show great versatility and restricted overhead coupled, employing appropriate setup tuning and execution enhancements. The work provisions critical points of interest of containerization.

The system [4] is an extensible copying system customized for Fog registering situations that empower without any preparation plan of Fog Computing foundations. It is also an imitation of authentic applications and outstanding burdens. EmuFog permits scientists to structure the system topology, as indicated by the utilization case. It inserts Fog Computing hubs in the topology and runs Docker-put together applications concerning those hubs associated with a copied system. Every one of the sub-modules of EmuFog is effectively extensible, though it gives a default execution to every one of them. The versatility and adequacy of EmuFog are assessed both on engineered and genuine system topologies.

The suggestion [5] is a hybrid fog and cloud interconnection system. It permits the programmed arrangement of cross-site virtual systems to interconnect topographically. It gives a flexible and multi-inhabitant positioning. It is a primitive and nonexclusive interface for starting up, designing, and sending Layer 2 and Layer 3 overlays. It organizes crosswise over the different fog and cloud stages, with reflection from the hidden cloud/fog innovations and advances of system virtualization.

Cirani *et al.* (2015) suggested [6] a Fog hub, indicated as IoT Hub. Its utilization at the edge of different systems improves the system's abilities by actualizing the accompanying capacities. The capacities include the fringe switch, cross-intermediary, reserve, and asset catalog. Execution of the IoT Hub provisions together a presentation assessment using IoT testbed.

Abedin *et al.* (2015) [7] addressed the utility-based coordinating or blending issue inside a similar area of IoT hubs. The authors utilized Irving's coordinating calculation under the device indicating inclinations to persevere through a stable IoT hub matching. The work [8] used the diagram dividing hypothesis to assemble the fog computation heap. It adjusted the calculation dependent on unique chart apportioning. The reproduction results showed that the structure of the fog processing after Cloud Atomization can fabricate the framework organization deftly. It can do a dynamic burden adjustment that can viably arrange framework assets just by decreasing the utilization of hub relocation brought by framework changes.

Steiner & Poledna (2016) [9] suggested an on-request reserving capacity virtualization plan and structure. The suggestion is a correspondence scheme between the fog hubs and the future Internet hubs for the sending procedure. The proposal controls the work virtualization approach to achieve smart control for related activities.

The suggestion [10] is another Fog computation worldview for business purposes. The primary thought is to bring the processing power from the remote Cloud nearer to the clients. The methodology further empowers ongoing communication and area-based administrations. Specifically, the nearby preparing ability of Fog registering altogether downsizes the information volume towards the Cloud, and its impacts affect the whole Internet.

Pop *et al.* (2018) [11] suggested a rundown booking based heuristic to tackle this issue. Shaik & Baskiyar (2018) [12] proposed a Hierarchical and Autonomous Fog Architecture (HAFA) to compose heterogeneous fog hubs into a multi-layered associated chain of command dependent on a few parameters. It makes additional clients, asset arrangements, protection, and security. Its gathering encourages asset pooling and neighborhood control. HAFA helps diminishing exertion in finding an ideal hub with required asset qualities towards administration organization.

Nodal Collaboration

Both edge and center systems are made by using the potential Fog processing framework. Ordinarily, these parts prepared with different sorts of processors are unfruitful for broadly useful registering. The arrangement oversees nodal cooperation among various fog hubs inside the edge organize.

Community Multi-gadget computation brings different advantages at various levels. At the client level, it fulfills the general need of individuals for joint effort and collaboration and makes a vivid client experience. At the application level, multi-gadget coordinated effort permits the trading of invaluable data. For instance, in regards to encompassing conditions during a fire danger for people on the call, it resolves the issue. At the framework level, it improves productivity by reusing calculation assets in the cloud, lessening end-to-end dormancy, sparing portable information use, *etc*.

Cost-Makespan aware Scheduling heuristic [13] proposal is significant to accomplish the harmony between the presentation of utilization execution and the mandatory expense for the utilization of cloud assets. The suggestion is a proficient reassignment technique dependent on the primary way of the coordinated non-cyclic diagram. The proposal refines the yield timetables of the Cost-Makespan aware Scheduling calculation to fulfill the client characterized cutoff time requirements or nature of administration of the framework.

Alsaffar *et al.* (2016) [14] recommended the design of IoT administration assignment and asset designation dependent on coordinated effort among fog and distributed computing. The creators propose calculation to apportion assets to meet the level of understanding and the nature of administrations just as to improve large information appropriation in fog and distributed computing. The work [15] is an insightful methodology that investigates the distributive and focal discernible stream system. It aims to evaluate the most basic recognizable occasions.

Resource/Service Provisioning Metric

Fog computation is a recently presented worldview, which stretches out the standard distributed computing to the edge. Along these lines, it is likewise called Edge Computing. It is a Micro Datacenter, profoundly virtualized stage, liable for giving calculation, stockpiling, and systems administration benefits between the end hubs in an IoT and customary fogs. Sensors, IoT hubs, gadgets, and Cloud Service Customers (CSC) contact to secure the required service at best case scenario cost. CSCs play out the arrangement and SLA assignments. When the agreement settles upon, the administration provides the same to the client. In such a manner, the system gives benefits on Adhoc premise, yet additionally, it needs to gauge utilization of assets, with the goal that they can be assigned ahead of time. Asset forecast permits more effectiveness and decency at the hour of usage. The components that add to the arrangement of assets and administrations productively are under various limitations.

The CloudSim toolbox [16] underpins both framework and conduct displaying of Cloud framework segments. Some examples include server farms, virtual machines (VMs), and asset provisioning arrangements. It actualizes conventional application provisioning procedures that can be stretched out and constrained effort. It bolsters displaying and recreation of Cloud processing situations comprising of both single and inter-networked fogs. Also, it uncovered custom interfaces for actualizing strategies and provisioning methods for the designation of VMs under inter-networked Cloud registering situations.

An autonomic controller, called FogQN-AC [17], changes the part of information handling successfully. The controller tries to upgrade a utility capacity of the regular reaction time and cost. This utility capacity utilizes a scientific reaction time and cost model recently created by the creators. The provision includes an appraisal of the controller against a savage power ideal arrangement. An exploratory evaluation of the controller utilizes engineered follows, Google follows, and a CityPulse savvy city street traffic dataset.

Gibson & Nguyen (2013) [18] built up a perceptually based difference improvement metric. This metric takes care of the issue related to self-governing upgrading pictures debased. A learning-based methodology builds up the complexity improvement utilizing human perceptions and low-level differentiation upgrade measurements dependent on the natural vision framework.

The suggestion [19] influenced an enormous scale, publicly supported following to handle three issues. It describes the vehicular traffic request, regarding generally speaking extent and substance separation. It evaluates how extraordinary reserving approaches perform against burden. It studies the impact of proposal frameworks and nearby substance things. The characterization is the cost of fog metric, communicating the extra reserving ability to convey while moving from customary, concentrated storing structures to a "fog processing" approach, where reserves are nearer to the system edge.

Jourani & Thibault (1995) [20] recommended a condition regarding restricting Fréchet subdifferentials [21]. It guarantees the metric consistency of a multivalued function considered. The creators apply the outcomes to the investigation of the restricting Fréchet subdifferential of a composite capacity characterized by a Banach space [22].

Namani & Kumar (2012) [23] characterized another coherence metric used to gauge the meaningfulness of given source code. From senior programming engineers, few principles were gathered, and afterward, these were concluded into a grade used to quantify the coherence of establishment. The portion of the current coherence measurements, for example, the Automated Readability Index (ARI), Gunning's Fox Index (FOG), and SMOG spontaneously executed. They are contrasting the consequences of these measurements with one another.

Fog Aware Density Evaluator (FADE) [24] predicts the permeability of a foggy scene from a separate picture without reference to a relating fog-free image. The technology works without reliance on significant items on the landscape without side land camera data, without assessing a profundity subordinate transmission map, and without preparing on human-appraised decisions. It utilizes quantifiable deviations from factual regularities. Fog critical highlights that characterize the perceptual fog thickness obtained from the space area NSS model and the watched attributes of foggy pictures. The system does not just predict perceptual fog thickness for the whole picture, but also gives a neighborhood fog thickness file. The anticipated fog thickness utilizes FADE associates well with human decisions of fog thickness taken in a non-technical report on an enormous foggy picture database. Another FADE-based referenceless is perceptual picture defogging, named DEnsity of Fog Assessment-based DEfogger (DEFADE). It accomplishes better outcomes for darker, denser foggy images.

Zhang *et al.* (2018) [25] proposed an expository structure of the offloading for registering systems. The plan includes an assignment delay and comparing vitality utilization. A planning metric is for each fog hub. A two-advance Fair Task Offloading (FTO) plot proposal chooses offloading fog hubs as indicated by the measure. The devices accept using offloads. It is dependent on a standard that limits of the errand delay.

Tarel *et al.* (2012) [26] reformulated the issue as the deduction of the nearby climatic cover. The calculation turns into a specific case. From this new inference, street pictures undergo analysis with an additional limitation. It considers an enormous piece of the images to be a planar street. The advantage of the system is the speed, the likelihood to deal with both shading and dim level pictures, and the modest number of parameters. Another plan proposal for rating permeability improvement calculations is dependent on the expansion of a few sorts of created on created and camera pictures.

Tandon & Simeone (2016) [27] suggestion depends on the presentation of a novel exhibition metric. The recommendation is Normalized Delivery Time (NDT) that quantifies the absolute conveyance inertness when contrasted with a perfect obstruction-free framework. A data is a hypothetically ideal portrayal of the exchange off between NDT, from one perspective, and fronthaul and storing assets. It infers for a class of fog Radio Access Network (F-RAN) with two edge hubs and two clients.

Khan *et al.* (2017) [28] presented a substance based centrality metric. It considers how well a hub is associated with the potential of the system it is conveying. The proposal [29] is a Quality analysis of experience-critical application situation arrangement. It organizes distinctive application position demands as indicated by client desires and computes the abilities of Fog. In Fog processing condition, it likewise uses to reasonable Fog occasions with the goal that client QoE undergoes augmented regarding utility access, asset utilization, and administration conveyance.

Service Level Objectives (SLO)

Availing service is a pattern of assembly between item-based ventures and administration segment. The gathering encompasses sensors, networks, and distributed computing as the fundamental empowering agents. The blend of servicing and sensors utilize the cloud system and fog processing standards are the primary models for novel arrangement. The gadgets closer to the edge are customarily not computationally good. It is enough to have every one of the modules of an application in the IoT biological system. Henceforth, the procedure should be defined in a manner that remembers these requirements, *i.e.*, repeats from the Fog layer towards the Cloud and attempts to put the modules first on the accessible assets on the Fog layer, from that point of repeating towards the Cloud. The SLOs achievement sends Fog processing as a middle of the road layer between Cloud datacenters and end gadgets/sensors.

Taneja & Davy (2017) [30] suggested a Module Mapping Algorithm for productive usage of assets in the system foundation. It was effectively conveying

Application Modules in Fog-Cloud Infrastructure for IoT based applications. With Fog registering into the picture, the calculation is dispersed successfully over the Fog and Cloud layer. The modules of an application would thus be able to be sent nearer to the source on gadgets in the Fog layer.

The methodology [31] is a test called iFogSim. It uses display IoT and Fog situations. It measures the effect of the asset. The assets include administrative procedures in dormancy organize blockage, vitality utilization, and cost. The work [32] presents the RECAP vision for an incorporated edge-cloud design. It talks about the logical establishment of the task and diagrams plans for toolsets. The constant information assortment, application execution demonstrating, application and segment auto-scaling and remediation, and arrangement advancement are using the toolsets.

The recommendation [33] depends on the idea of virtual and physical networks, and it has just indicated its effectiveness when applied to distributed computing. Shekhar *et al.* (2017) [34] suggested the INDICES structure that restricts by giving a novel arrangement. The positioning decides when and to which Micro Datacenters (MDC) assistance movement to and along these lines provides the ideal execution.

Applicable Network System

Fog Computing places the customary cloud benefits nearer to the end-clients offering different advantages. Some of the examples include low inactivity, area awareness, and portability support. It coordinates with Core Cloud administrations, transforms traditional server holdings into circulated heterogeneous stages. Computing, accordingly, underpins Internet of Thing (IoT) applications in vehicle systems, and sensors. The modern computerization requires delicate postponement and preparation. To privilege Fog Calculation is an arrangement required to oversee assets and administrations crosswise over edge gadgets. Fog administrations are provisioned and followed among the devices. It is a unique systems administration framework where Fog registering presentation is the expansion of other registering ideal models.

Wang *et al.* (2017) [35] coordinated fog computation into data-driven Internet of Vehicles (IoV) to give versatility support. The assistance provisions distribute distinctive patterns and assess the information trademark. Sengupta *et al.* (2018) [36] offered a model to order scientific categorizations of the entire arrangement of assets intended to best suit the Fog-to-Cloud (F2C) worldview.

The approach [37] is to bring functionalities as near the gadgets as could be expected under the circumstances to diminish dormancy and improve information security and correspondence power. Toczé & Nadjm-Tehrani (2018) [38] portrayed current works inside the field of edge computation. The work [39] is a changed Stable Election Protocol (SEP), named Prolong-SEP (P-SEP). Its exhibition draws out the steady time of Fog-bolstered sensor organization by keeping up adjusted vitality utilization. P-SEP empowers uniform hubs conveyance, new cluster head choosing approach. It also draws out the time interim of the framework. P-SEP thinks about two-level heterogeneity - progressed and ordinary devices. In P-SEP, the progressed and typical hubs have the chance to become cluster heads.

Brito *et al.* (2017) [40] proposed a design for Orchestration for the Fog Computing condition. It presents Architecture for administration coordination dependent on the center necessities of Fog Computing. A virtualized situation aids the functioning of the Fog Nodes. They are containerized applications and administrations, offering them access to appended/associated gadgets, over various correspondence advancements, to achieve their errands.

Security Concern

Thota *et al.* (2018) [41] proposed a secure design incorporated in IoT based medicinal services framework conveyed in Cloud condition. The proposal utilizes Fog Computing conditions to run the structure. The well-being information is gathered from sensors and safely sent to edge gadgets. The gadgets move the information to the cloud system for consistent access by human services experts. Security and protection for patient medicinal data are critical for the acknowledgment. The fundamental focal point of this work is to verify the Authentication and Authorization of a considerable number of gadgets. The system identifies and Tracks the devices conveyed in the framework, Locates the cell phones, new things arrangement and association with the existing structure, Communicates among the gadgets and information move between remote human services frameworks. The proposed framework utilizes non-concurrent correspondence between the applications and information servers conveyed in the cloud condition.

The proposal [42] screens information access in the cloud system and recognizes strange information. On unapproved access, it suspects and afterward checks by querying challenge questions. The system dispatches disinformation assault by returning a lot of fake data to the assailant. The creators utilize this innovation to dispatch disinformation assaults against malignant insiders. It secures against the abuse of the client's authentic information. The creators propose two different ways of utilizing Fog processing to anticipate attacks. For example, in the Twitter system sending fake data inside the Cloud by the Cloud administration client can be considered.

Dsouza *et al.* (2014) [43] proposed an arrangement-based administration of assets in fog processing. The system involves growing the present fog registering stage to help secure coordinated effort, and interoperability between various clients mentioned assets in fog computation. The arrangement of the board module commitment helps the organization layer of fog engineering. The foremost part of the calculation happens inside the fog hubs. The all-encompassing plan comprises modules wherein every module plays a particular and definitive job. It can be connected and played continuously. It is dependent on setups characterized by executives of comparing facilitated applications and the proprietor of a specific fog condition.

Fog computing based context-aware filtering for security services (FCSS) [44] is data-driven informal organizations. The FCSS has the evaluation and coordinating plans and the fog processing scheme for security benefits using Information-Centric Sensor Network (ICSN). The fog registers with ICSN. The arrangement gives low-idleness to security administration sifting and assists from start to finish. Secondly, a content-mark innovation-based proficient plan suggestion acknowledges precise separation for security administrations.

Hu *et al.* (2017) [45] suggested a security and protection safeguarding plan. The layout of the fog registration has its basis in face distinguishing proof. The confirmation and session key understanding plan, information encryption plan, and information trustworthiness checking plan follows. This method aims in uprightness and accessibility in the procedures to recognize face proof and face goals.

Rivest–Shamir–Adleman (RSA) algorithm [46] and Elliptic-curve cryptography (ECC) [47] are proportionate security levels [48]. The work analyzes power utilization and information throughput using a testbed of IoT entryways. The work [49] gives a security system fusing inescapable and wearable registering, IoT, clouds, and fog computation to defend people and block any setback. The creators have used a layered methodology having different layers with expanding the level of complexity. It guarantees that the most functional choice is set aside in the least measure of effort for every situation. The recommendation [50] is a triparty one-round validated key understanding convention. It has been proposed depending on the bilinear matching cryptography that can create a session key among the members and impart them safely. The private human services information is gotten to and put away with safety by executing a baiting procedure. The procedure introduces verifying the patient's Multiple Breath

Washout (MBD) in the human services cloud utilizing the bait strategy with a fog computation office. It fills in as a subsequent exhibition to contain baits that appear to the assailant as though it is the first MBD. In the proposal, the bait records are recovered from the earliest starting point to guarantee better security. Furthermore, it utilizes a twofold security strategy by scrambling the first document when an aggressor perceives that he/she is managing a fake exhibition.

Hamid *et al.* (2017) [51] addressed this issue by proposing another idea. The work expands the calculation and capacity intensity of fog registering. The proposal of a creative methodology named Fog Vehicle Computing (FVC) upgrades the adaptability of a fog registering foundation. FVC exploits a unique gathering of vehicles to support the computational power and decline in the dormancy of fog computation. The possibility of FVC offers favorable circumstances for both fog specialist cooperation and the vehicle proprietors.

FUTURE DIRECTIONS

Examination of various methods to apply logical data in asset and administration of the board can be a potential field towards Fog based approach-

- Maintaining the Fog registering streamlines and its financial and ecological impact. The unwavering quality in Fog computation improves with the consistency of Fog gestures, accessibility of elite administrations, verified collaborations, adaptation to internal failure, and so on.

- Fog hubs need to perform more computation instead of a systems administration doings. Subsequently, an interoperable design of Fog hubs that can act naturally altered by the prerequisites is exceptionally fundamental.

- Fog hubs undergo circulation over the edge. The issues viewing disseminate application arrangement, for example, inactivity management, dataflow of the executives, QoS affirmation, and edge-driven liking of ongoing applications.

- Fog hubs need to manage an enormous number of administration demands originating from the end gadgets/sensors at the same time. In this manner, while reacting to the number of administration demands, appropriate power w.r.t the executives inside Fog organization is vital.

- Accessible assets of Fog hubs can be virtualized and apportioned to various users. The multi-occupant support in Fog assets and booking the calculation undertakings indicated by their QoS prerequisites requires detailed exploration.

- The estimating and charging strategies in Fog differ altogether from the Cloud arranged approaches. Because of the absence of appropriate estimate and charging approaches of Fog based administrations, frequently clients face trouble in distinguishing reasonable suppliers for directing SLA.

Dsouza *et al.* (2014) [43] suggested addressing an advanced method to recognize arrangement clashes and resolve the identified conflict. They characterized a lot of inconsistencies that tend in fog computation conditions. The use of cases of assorted gadgets can gauge the adequacy of the methodology with the increasingly practical testbed. Sehgal *et al.* (2015) [49] suggested handling the security and moral worries that surface because of individual data included. Hamid *et al.* (2017) [51] recommended taking up Task planning as the most significant prerequisites to improve the productivity of FVC.

REFERENCES

[1]   F. Hany, "Fog Computing and the Internet of Things: A Review", *big data and cognitive computing,* vol. 2, no. 2, pp. 1-18, June 2018.

[2]   R. Mahmud, R. Kotagiri, and R. Buyya, Fog computing: A taxonomy, survey and future directions. *Internet of Everything.,* B. Di Martino, Ed., Springer: Singapore, Singapore, 2018, pp. 103-130. [http://dx.doi.org/10.1007/978-981-10-5861-5_5]

[3]   P. Bellavista, and A. Zanni, "Feasibility of fog computing deployment based on docker containerization over raspberrypi", In: *18ᵗʰ international conference on distributed computing and networking*, Hyderabad, India, 2017, pp. 1-10. [http://dx.doi.org/10.1145/3007748.3007777]

[4]   R. Mayer, L. Graser, H. Gupta, E. Saurez, and U. Ramachandran, "Emufog: Extensible and scalable emulation of large-scale fog computing infrastructures", *IEEE Fog World Congress (FWC),* 2017, pp. 1-6 Santa Clara, CA, USA. [http://dx.doi.org/10.1109/FWC.2017.8368525]

[5]   R. Moreno-Vozmediano, R.S. Montero, E. Huedo, and I.M. Llorente, "Cross-site virtual network in cloud and fog computing", *IEEE Cloud Computing,* vol. 4, no. 2, pp. 46-53, 2017. [http://dx.doi.org/10.1109/MCC.2017.28]

[6]   S. Cirani, G. Ferrari, N. Iotti, and M. Picone, "The iot hub: a fog node for seamless management of heterogeneous connected smart objects", *12th Annual IEEE International Conference on Sensing, Communication, and Networking-Workshops (SECON Workshops),* 2015, pp. 1-6 Seattle, WA, USA. [http://dx.doi.org/10.1109/SECONW.2015.7328145]

[7]   S.F. Abedin, M.G.R. Alam, N.H. Tran, and C.S. Hong, "A Fog based system model for cooperative IoT node pairing using matching theory", *17ᵗʰ Asia-Pacific Network Operations and Management Symposium (APNOMS),* 2015, pp. 309-314 Busan, South Korea. [http://dx.doi.org/10.1109/APNOMS.2015.7275445]

[8]   S. Ningning, G. Chao, A. Xingshuo, and Z. Qiang, "Fog computing dynamic load balancing mechanism based on graph repartitioning", *China Commun.,* vol. 13, no. 3, pp. 156-164, 2016. [http://dx.doi.org/10.1109/CC.2016.7445510]

[9]   W. Steiner, and S. Poledna, "Fog computing as enabler for the Industrial Internet of Things", *e & i Elektrotechnik und Informationstechnik,* vol. 133, no. 7, pp. 310-314, October 2016. [http://dx.doi.org/10.1007/s00502-016-0438-2]

[10] J. Li, J. Jin, D. Yuan, M. Palaniswami, and K. Moessner, "EHOPES: Data-centered Fog platform for

smart living", *2015 International Telecommunication Networks and Applications Conference (ITNAC),* 2015, pp. 308-313 Sydney, NSW, Australia.
[http://dx.doi.org/10.1109/ATNAC.2015.7366831]

[11]   P. Pop, M.L. Raagaard, M. Gutierrez, and W. Steiner, "Enabling fog computing for industrial automation through time-sensitive networking (TSN)", *IEEE Communications Standards Magazine,* vol. 2, no. 2, pp. 55-61, 2018.
[http://dx.doi.org/10.1109/MCOMSTD.2018.1700057]

[12]   S. Shaik, and S. Baskiyar, "Hierarchical and Autonomous Fog Architecture", *47th International Conference on Parallel Processing Companion,* 2018, p. 18 Eugene, OR, USA.

[13]   X.Q. Pham, N.D. Man, N.D.T. Tri, N.Q. Thai, and E.N. Huh, "A cost-and performance-effective approach for task scheduling based on collaboration between cloud and fog computing", *Int. J. Distrib. Sens. Netw.,* vol. 13, no. 11, pp. 1-16, 2017.
[http://dx.doi.org/10.1177/1550147717742073]

[14]   A.A. Alsaffar, H.P. Pham, C.S. Hong, E.N. Huh, and M. Aazam, "An architecture of iot service delegation and resource allocation based on collaboration between fog and cloud computing", *Mobile Information Systems,* vol. 2016, pp. 1-15, 2016.
[http://dx.doi.org/10.1155/2016/6123234]

[15]   R.Y. Chen, "An intelligent value stream-based approach to collaboration of food traceability cyber physical system by fog computing", *Food Control,* vol. 71, pp. 124-136, 2017.
[http://dx.doi.org/10.1016/j.foodcont.2016.06.042]

[16]   R.N. Calheiros, R. Ranjan, A. Beloglazov, C.A. De Rose, and R. Buyya, "CloudSim: a toolkit for modeling and simulation of cloud computing environments and evaluation of resource provisioning algorithms", *Softw. Pract. Exper.,* vol. 41, no. 1, pp. 23-50, 2011.
[http://dx.doi.org/10.1002/spe.995]

[17]   U. Tadakamalla, and D.A. Menascé, "Autonomic resource management using analytic models for fog/cloud computing", *IEEE International Conference on Fog Computing (ICFC),* 2019, pp. 69-79 Prague, Czech Republic.
[http://dx.doi.org/10.1109/ICFC.2019.00018]

[18]   K.B. Gibson, and T.Q. Nguyen, "A no-reference perceptual based contrast enhancement metric for ocean scenes in fog", *IEEE Trans. Image Process.,* vol. 22, no. 10, pp. 3982-3993, 2013.
[http://dx.doi.org/10.1109/TIP.2013.2265884] [PMID: 23744681]

[19]   F. Malandrino, C. Chiasserini, and S. Kirkpatrick, "The price of fog: A data-driven study on caching architectures in vehicular networks", *First International Workshop on Internet of Vehicles and Vehicles of Internet,* 2016, pp. 37-42 Paderborn, Germany.
[http://dx.doi.org/10.1145/2938681.2938682]

[20]   A. Jourani, and L. Thibault, "Metric regularity and subdifferential calculus in Banach spaces", *Set-Valued Anal.,* vol. 3, no. 1, pp. 87-100, 1995.
[http://dx.doi.org/10.1007/BF01033643]

[21]   A.Y. Kruger, "On fréchet subdifferentials", *J. Math. Sci.,* vol. 116, no. 3, pp. 3325-3358, 2003.
[http://dx.doi.org/10.1023/A:1023673105317]

[22]   F.E. Browder, "Nonexpansive nonlinear operators in a Banach space", *Nat. Acad. Sci. USA, US,* vol. 54,4, pp. 1041-1044, 1965.
[http://dx.doi.org/10.1073/pnas.54.4.1041]

[23]   R. Namani, and J. Kumar, "A new metric for code readability", *IOSR J. Comp. Eng.,* vol. 6, no. 6, pp. 44-48, 2012.
[http://dx.doi.org/10.9790/0661-0664448]

[24]   L.K. Choi, J. You, and A.C. Bovik, "Referenceless prediction of perceptual fog density and perceptual image defogging", *IEEE Trans. Image Process.,* vol. 24, no. 11, pp. 3888-3901, 2015.

[http://dx.doi.org/10.1109/TIP.2015.2456502] [PMID: 26186784]

[25]   G. Zhang, F. Shen, Y. Yang, H. Qian, and W. Yao, "Fair task offloading among fog nodes in fog computing networks", *IEEE International Conference on Communications (ICC)*, 2018, pp. 1-6 Kansas City, MO, USA.
[http://dx.doi.org/10.1109/ICC.2018.8422316]

[26]   J.P. Tarel, "Vision enhancement in homogeneous and heterogeneous fog", *IEEE Intel. Trans. Sys. Mag.*, vol. 4, no. 2, pp. 6-20, 2012.
[http://dx.doi.org/10.1109/MITS.2012.2189969]

[27]   R. Tandon, and O. Simeone, "Cloud-aided wireless networks with edge caching: Fundamental latency trade-offs in fog radio access networks", *IEEE International Symposium on Information Theory (ISIT)*, 2016, pp. 2029-2033 Barcelona, Spain.
[http://dx.doi.org/10.1109/ISIT.2016.7541655]

[28]   J.A. Khan, C. Westphal, and Y. Ghamri-Doudane, "A content-based centrality metric for collaborative caching in information-centric fogs", *IFIP Networking Conference (IFIP Networking) and Workshops*, 2017, pp. 1-6 Stockholm, Sweden.
[http://dx.doi.org/10.23919/IFIPNetworking.2017.8264869]

[29]   R. Mahmud, S.N. Srirama, K. Ramamohanarao, and R. Buyya, "Quality of Experience (QoE)-aware placement of applications in Fog computing environments", *J. Parallel Distrib. Comput.*, vol. 132, pp. 190-203, 2019.
[http://dx.doi.org/10.1016/j.jpdc.2018.03.004]

[30]   M. Taneja, and A. Davy, "Resource aware placement of IoT application modules in Fog-Cloud Computing Paradigm", *IFIP/IEEE Symposium on Integrated Network and Service Management (IM)*, 2017, pp. 1222-1228 Lisbon, Portugal.
[http://dx.doi.org/10.23919/INM.2017.7987464]

[31]   H. Gupta, A. Vahid Dastjerdi, S.K. Ghosh, and R. Buyya, "iFogSim: A toolkit for modeling and simulation of resource management techniques in the Internet of Things, Edge and Fog computing environments", *Softw. Pract. Exper.*, vol. 47, no. 9, pp. 1275-1296, 2017.
[http://dx.doi.org/10.1002/spe.2509]

[32]   P.O. Östberg, "Reliable capacity provisioning for distributed cloud/edge/fog computing applications", *2017 European conference on networks and communications (EuCNC)*, 2017, pp. 1-6 Oulu, Finland.
[http://dx.doi.org/10.1109/EuCNC.2017.7980667]

[33]   S. Filiposka, A. Mishev, and K. Gilly, "Community-based allocation and migration strategies for fog computing", *IEEE Wireless Communications and Networking Conference (WCNC)*, 2018, pp. 1-6 Barcelona, Spain.
[http://dx.doi.org/10.1109/WCNC.2018.8377095]

[34]   S. Shekhar, A.D. Chhokra, A. Bhattacharjee, G. Aupy, and A. Gokhale, "Indices: exploiting edge resources for performance-aware cloud-hosted services", In: *IEEE 1st International Conference on Fog and Edge Computing (ICFEC)*, Madrid, Spain, 2017, pp. 75-80.
[http://dx.doi.org/10.1109/ICFEC.2017.16]

[35]   M. Wang, "Toward mobility support for information-centric IoV in smart city using fog computing", *IEEE International Conference on Smart Energy Grid Engineering (SEGE)*, 2017, pp. 357-361 Oshawa, ON, Canada.
[http://dx.doi.org/10.1109/SEGE.2017.8052825]

[36]   S. Sengupta, J. Garcia, and X. Masip-Bruin, "Taxonomy and resource modeling in combined fog-t-
-cloud systems", *Future Technologies Conference*, 2018, pp. 687-704 Vancouver, Canada.

[37]   M.S. De Brito, S. Hoque, R. Steinke, and A. Willner, "Towards programmable fog nodes in smart factories", In: *1st International Workshops on Foundations and Applications of Self* Systems.* Augsburg, Germany, 2016, pp. 236-241.

[38]   K. Toczé, and S. Nadjm-Tehrani, "A taxonomy for management and optimization of multiple resources in edge computing", *Wirel. Commun. Mob. Comput.,* 2018.
[http://dx.doi.org/10.1155/2018/7476201]

[39]   P.G.V. Naranjo, M. Shojafar, H. Mostafaei, Z. Pooranian, and E. Baccarelli, "P-SEP: A prolong stable election routing algorithm for energy-limited heterogeneous fog-supported wireless sensor networks", *J. Supercomput.,* vol. 73, no. 2, pp. 733-755, 2017.
[http://dx.doi.org/10.1007/s11227-016-1785-9]

[40]   M. Santos de Brito, "A service orchestration architecture for Fog-enabled infrastructures", *Second International Conference on Fog and Mobile Edge Computing (FMEC),* 2017, pp. 127-132 Valencia, Spain.
[http://dx.doi.org/10.1109/FMEC.2017.7946419]

[41]   C. Thota, R. Sundarasekar, G. Manogaran, R. Varatharajan, and M.K. Priyan, Centralized fog computing security platform for IoT and cloud in healthcare system.*Fog Computing: Breakthroughs in Research and Practice.,* C. Thota, Ed., IGI global: India, 2018, pp. 365-378.
[http://dx.doi.org/10.4018/978-1-5225-5649-7.ch018]

[42]   S.J. Stolfo, M.B. Salem, and A.D. Keromytis, "Fog computing: Mitigating insider data theft attacks in the cloud", In: *IEEE symposium on security and privacy workshops*, San Francisco, CA, USA, 2012, pp. 125-128.
[http://dx.doi.org/10.1109/SPW.2012.19]

[43]   C. Dsouza, G.J. Ahn, and M. Taguinod, "Policy-driven security management for fog computing: Preliminary framework and a case study", In: *IEEE 15th International Conference on Information Reuse and Integration (IEEE IRI 2014)*, Redwood City, CA, USA, 2014, pp. 16-23.
[http://dx.doi.org/10.1109/IRI.2014.7051866]

[44]   J. Wu, M. Dong, K. Ota, J. Li, and Z. Guan, "FCSS: Fog computing based content-aware filtering for security services in information centric social networks", *IEEE Trans. Emerg. Top. Comput.,* vol. 7, no. 4, pp. 553-564, 2017.
[http://dx.doi.org/10.1109/TETC.2017.2747158]

[45]   P. Hu, "Security and privacy preservation scheme of face identification and resolution framework using fog computing in internet of things", *IEEE Inter. Things J.,* vol. 4, no. 5, pp. 1143-1155, 2017.
[http://dx.doi.org/10.1109/JIOT.2017.2659783]

[46]   P.C. Kocher, "Timing attacks on implementations of Diffie-Hellman, RSA, DSS, and other systems", *Annual International Cryptology Conference,* 1996, pp. 104-113 Santa Barbara, California, USA.
[http://dx.doi.org/10.1007/3-540-68697-5_9]

[47]   Z. Jia, Y. Zhang, H. Shao, Y. Lin, and J. Wang, "A Remote User Authentication Scheme Using Bilinear Pairings and ECC", *Proceedings of the Sixth International Conference on Intelligent Systems Design and Applications (ISDA '06),* 2006, pp. 1091-1094 Jinan, China.
[http://dx.doi.org/10.1109/ISDA.2006.253764]

[48]   M. Suárez-Albela, T.M. Fernández-Caramés, P. Fraga-Lamas, and L. Castedo, "A practical evaluation of a high-security energy-efficient gateway for IoT fog computing applications", *Sensors (Basel),* vol. 17, no. 9, p. 1978, 2017.
[http://dx.doi.org/10.3390/s17091978] [PMID: 28850104]

[49]   V. K. Sehgal, A. Patrick, A. Soni, and L. Rajput, "Smart human security framework using internet of things, cloud and fog computing", *Intelligent distributed computing,* vol. 321, pp. 251-263, October 2015.
[http://dx.doi.org/10.1007/978-3-319-11227-5_22]

[50]   M. Sookhak, "Fog vehicular computing: Augmentation of fog computing using vehicular cloud computing", *IEEE Veh. Technol. Mag.,* vol. 12, no. 3, pp. 55-64, 2017.
[http://dx.doi.org/10.1109/MVT.2017.2667499]

[51]　Al Hamid, "A security model for preserving the privacy of medical big data in a healthcare cloud using a fog computing facility with pairing-based cryptography", *IEEE Access,* vol. 5, pp. 22313-22328, 2017.
[http://dx.doi.org/10.1109/ACCESS.2017.2757844]

CHAPTER 5

Integration of IoT and Cloud Computing

Abstract: The Internet of Things (IoT) is a self-configuring device interconnected in a dynamic and worldwide system foundation. Such devices actualize the monitoring process by little things assistance deployed in the environment. However, they carry out their tasks with restricted stockpiling and handling limits. Other concerns include activities related to unwavering quality, execution, security, and protection. Cloud has boundless abilities with ample capacity and data preparation. It has substantially more experienced innovation for handling the majority of the IoT issues. A novel IT worldview in which Cloud and IoT are two reciprocal advances consolidated and relied upon to build the future. The following chapter summarizes the integrated system, its applications and contribution. It also discusses some of the open issues of the technology.

Keywords: Applications, Characteristics, Cloud-IoT, Integration.

INTRODUCTION

With the far-reaching accessibility using the remote Internet, these scaled-down electronic gadgets procure availability with minimal effort. It is conceivable to envision the Internet extended to incorporate items, installed with sensors, imparting over the Internet in tremendous numbers. These items are normal physical things that are enlarged by a PC incorporating a sensor or actuator and a specialized gadget. CloudIoT brought forth another arrangement of shrewd administrations and applications that can firmly affect regular day to day existence. A significant number of the applications have been portrayed in the accompanying advantage from Machine-to-Machine interchanges when the things need to trade data among themselves and not just send them towards the cloud. Fig. (**1**) represents cloud-IoT architecture.

CHARACTERISTICS OF INTEGRATION

The Internet of Things (IoT) depends on savvy and self-arranging devices interconnected in a dynamic and worldwide system foundation.

Ambika Nagaraj

It is concerned with one of the most problematic advancements, empowering universal and unavoidable registering situations. IoT is portrayed by certifiable little things that are broadly disseminated, with constrained capacity and preparing limit. Cloud registering has boundless abilities with ample capacity and preparation. It also has some problems to be resolved - dependability, execution, security, and protection. A novel IT prototype in which Cloud and IoT are two integral advancements consolidated.This new Prototype convention is named CloudIoT. The following section summarizes the contributions made towards the amalgamation of the two.

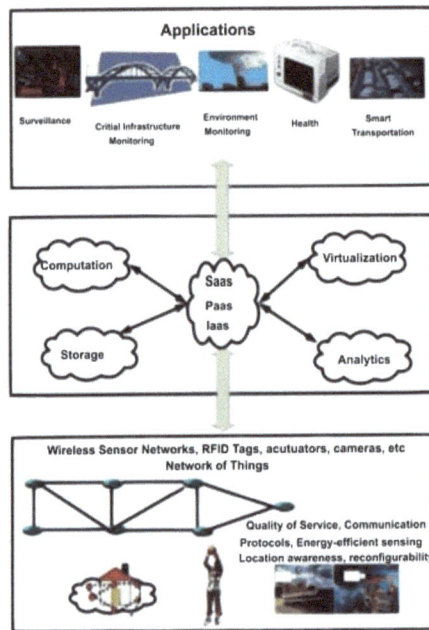

Fig. (1). Cloud-centric IoT Architecture [1].

Scalable

From a keen city administration arrangement viewpoint, IoT gadgets always make their administrations available at the city cloud level. The intrigued outsider savvy city applications (*e.g.*, traffic checking frameworks) will make use of these administrations dependent on conventions for administration revelation and their inclinations as far as nature of administration necessities. Among a few difficulties emerging in this situation, there exist two troubles that require some solution. To start with, the nearness of a large number of smart and irregular gadgets in urban communities, a significant need is a versatile method to show and uncover IoT administrations at the Cloud that guarantees simple, quick conveyance of keen city administrations. Second, the occasion driven nature of Administrations in IoT frameworks requires a component for the arrangement of administrations in actual world doings.

Taherkordi & Eliassen [2] recommended conventional IoT administration for display. The system is explicitly intended for huge scale cloud-based IoT applications, for example, smart urban communities. The embodiment of the methodology is organizing the portrayal of IoT benefits in the various leveled model. They populated them in a tree structure containing references to administrations and their actual world information channels. The general plan approach is an adaptable tree-based model. It helps to get to show in which every device of the tree is made dependent on developing relevant parameters of the IoT application. *e.g.*, the area set for a brilliant city can be hierarchized from a significant level city metropolitan locale down to neighborhoods and roads. The creators implemented the work using Firebase as the platform. It is a cloud-based, ongoing back-end framework that permitted to construct different information handling highlights in real-time. Information in a Firebase database is put away as JSON and synchronized to each associated customer. Bellavista & Zanni [3] proposed creative circulated engineering joining machine-to-machine industry-develop conventions. It is a unique method to upgrade the versatility of entryways for proficient IoT-cloud coordination. The implementation used the RaspberryPi model B+ and Parallel VM (512MB RAM, single-core CPU, Xubuntu OS).

Storage

A study introduces an information accumulation system [4]. It is empowering and proficiently put away enormous IoT information and also incorporate both organized and unstructured knowledge. This collection system can join and stretch out numerous databases like Hadoop to store and oversee differing information gathered by sensors and RFID perusers. A contextual investigation is considered to break down the work. Many coordination orders are followed by IoT-based advancements, for example, RFID peruses, sensors, and cameras. The information produced by the gadgets is first gathered and preprocessed by some terminals and afterward sent to a coordinator of the board application. The construction is dependent on the information stockpiling structure. This method improves the exhibition of information put away and inserted. A wide range of information is put away in better places utilizing MySQL database, Mongo-DB, and record archives.

An operational procedure is suggested [5], which encourages the legal specialist to consider the most recent BitTorrent Sync applications. The network was provided with comprehensive ancient rarities that are probably going to stay after the utilization of the more up to date BitTorrent Sync cloud applications is adopted. Two Virtual Machines (VMs) are used for each working framework explored to speak to the host and the visitor workstations. An aggregate of 24 VM depictions of every workstation speaking to 24 verified situations of utilizing BitTorrent Sync was used. To forgo examination into the portable applications, a default industrial facility reestablished iPhone 4 running iOS 7.1.2, and an HTC One X running Android KitKat 4.4.4 was arranged. The creators have considered rooting both the gadgets utilizing Pangu8 v1.1 and Odin3 v.185 to empower root, separately.

Another system [6] enables an association to transfer IoT information safely in an open cloud. The transfer includes hierarchical data allocation of data on the private cloud. The actualized methodology gives extraordinary productivity during encryption and decoding of the message. The actualized framework is valuable in different business associations. In these systems, the information gathered from IoT gadgets and occupation functionalities is isolated by the tasks performed by the client in organizations. The gathered data from IoT gadgets are safely transferred to distributed storage by upholding AES and RSA cryptographic methods. Three unique machines are used to demonstrate the procedure. It is evaluated for encryption of DES, AES, AES, and RSA calculation on the diverse bundle size on the I3 framework having 2 GB RAM.

Fazio *et al.* [7] suggested engineering that consolidates the advantages of stockpiling. Specifically, it enables us to expand SQL-like heritage frameworks, and then to oversee Big Data through an XML-like, non-SQL dispersed stockpiling structure as per a Cloud organization approach. The entire structure depends on a data-centric method. This method permits to rearrange non-concurrent correspondences between checking situations and end-clients.

The suggested [8] structure is adaptable and conservative. The design takes care of the storage issues by coordinating with the fog. During time idleness, the gathered information is handled and put away by the edge server or the cloud server. The procedure starts with the refinement of knowledge by the edge server, and afterward, the time-critical information is utilized and put away locally. The non-time-critical information is transmitted to the cloud server to help information recovery and mining at the later stage. An RF tree and an ID-AVL tree played the role of an intermediary server. The RF tree encoding by the safe kNN procedure adds security to the system. The devices speak with one another by the ZigBee convention. The creators utilize a PC with a 2.6 GHz Intel Core processor,

Window 7 activity framework, and a RAM of 4 GB to go about as an edge server. A personal computer with a 3.6 GHz Intel Core processor, Windows 7 working framework, and a RAM of 8 GB was used as the cloud server.

APPLICATIONS

The combined technology is made useful in many applications. The section contains the suggestions provided by various authors in diverse applications.

Healthcare

Kum *et al.* [9] recommended a novel system to participate in cloud-level IoT benefits [10] on a keen gadget with the idea of Intention. The work characterizes the techniques to depict the aim of the customer, relating it with different clients. The proposed system utilizes IoT Device Delegate to control every gadget from numerous clouds and Intention Manager to oversee the connection between gadgets. On an i7-based PC, the creators have set up an HTTP server with Apache and Tomcat and executed IoT Device Delegate for five gadgets from 3 cloud-scale IoT administrations- Smart Things, Weather Station, and Withings. Gadgets are entryway, vicinity and climate sensors, electrical plug, and lights. IoT Device Delegate can provide data for every gadget and state three cloud-level IoT benefits, and make Data Channel for each of them by employing HTTP. Long surveying and AJAX are utilized to obtain them. Each datum Channel has successively refreshed information from gadget/administration and introduced them in the HTML program on PC, and WebApp advanced mobile phone and SmartTV.

The design of an ECG observing framework [11] proposal is dependent on the Internet-of-Things (IoT) cloud. The ECG information assembled from the human body will be transmitted straightforwardly to the IoT-cloud utilizing Wi-Fi without the need for a versatile terminal. The accumulated data is put away in a non-social database, which can enormously improve the speed and adaptability of information stockpiling. An actualized online graphical UI provides straightforward entry to specialists and patients. They utilize the same PDAs of various OS stages to access the information offered by the IoT-cloud.

Another proposal [12] employs diabetes sicknesses and related restorative information. The production is made possible by utilizing the UCI Repository dataset and the medicinal sensors for foreseeing the individuals who have been influenced by diabetes harshly. The creators propose another grouping calculation called the Fuzzy Rule-based Neural Classifier for diagnosing the ailment and seriousness. Four distinct classifiers, for example, Decision Tree (DT), k-Nearest Neighbor (k-NN), Naïve Bayes (NB), and Support Vector Machine (SVM) are utilized for diagnosing the maladies.

Jabbar, Ullah, Khalid, Khan, & Han [13] recommended an IoT based Semantic Interoperability Model (IoT-SIM). The system gives Semantic Interoperability among diversified IoT gadgets in the medicinal services area. Doctors discuss their patients with heterogeneous IoT gadgets to screen their present wellbeing status. Data among doctors and patients is semantically commented on and conveyed in a noteworthy manner. The suggestion is a lightweight model for semantic explanation of information utilizing diversified gadgets in IoT. Asset Description Framework (RDF) is a semantic web system that employs to relate things that are using triples to make it semantically significant.

The work [14] based on kHealth is a customized computerized medicinal services data framework that is being created and tried for checking illness. The significant application features of IoT-based wellbeing informatics structures include redistributed calculations and data sharing. Re-appropriated computation identification with everything takes place with client information outside the border of their gadgets and home systems.

The system [15] introduces a portable entryway design in which the primary reason for existance is to get the detecting information and make a nearby investigation. It creates catchphrases and sends it to the remote therapeutic server for examination.

The work [16] is the understudy of serious sickness. The detection is analyzed by foreseeing the potential ailment with its level by transiently mining the wellbeing estimations gathered from medicinal and other IoT gadgets. The suggestion is a building model for savvy understudy of the human services framework. The information is divided to approve the model by utilizing the k-cross approval approach. The experiments are checked genuinely by looking at understudy wellbeing manifestations procured from UCI information archive and sensor estimation information with suitable finding rule. The WEKA Toolkit is used to analyze information mining tasks. The creators have received an application by transforming it into administration parts characterized by the Web Service Resource Framework (WSRF) models. An outsider cloud like Amazon EC2 for information examination is employed. It is an Infrastructure as an assistance (IaaS) supplier that helps in creating different sorts of machine occurrences. A distinctive Amazon Machine Image (AMI) with default example "m1.small" is picked to run on CentOS 6.7 with a Linux 2.6.32Xen Kernel.

Smart Environment

The Smart environment is related to the inescapability of system inclusion and inserted registering advancements in accepting a consistently developing centrality for individuals living in the profoundly created zones. The heterogeneity of gadgets, administrations, correspondence conventions, benchmarks and information positions engaged with the vast majority of the accessible arrangements created by various merchants, is unfavorably influencing its far-reaching application. Distributed computing has likewise been utilized to reshape home administrations and applications in the home mechanization area. Furthermore, gadgets from various sellers are successively furnished with on-board modules that can reach the Internet. The new arrangements rose to incorporate existing systems, different sensors, on-board modules in gadgets, entryways, and distributed computing have made shrewd environment-situated clouds.

The work [17] is a novel multi-layer cloud structural model. It empowers powerful and consistent connections/interoperations on diversified gadgets/administrations given by various merchants in an IoT-based savvy home. The utilization illuminates the heterogeneity issues in the introduced layered cloud stage. The methodology is a promising method to address information portrayal, information, and application heterogeneity. It is a philosophy based security administration system intended for supporting security and protection conservation during the time spent on communications/interoperations. The implementation model compris an open cloud provided by Amazon EC2. It is a personal brilliant home cloud stage bolstered by Guangdong University Scientific Innovation Project and implicit Dongguan University of Technology (DGUT), and a keen home cloud stage approved by Canbo CO., LTD, China.

Suciu, *et al.* [18] have recommended another stage for utilizing distributed computing capacitics concerning arrangement and backing of pervasive availability and ongoing applications and administrations for smart urban community's needs. The creators present a structure for information acquired from exceptionally disseminated, heterogeneous, decentralized, genuine, and virtual gadgets. These gadgets can be overseen, dissected, and constrained by dispersed cloud-based administrations.

Pacheco & Hariri [19] have presented an IoT security system for Intelligent structures. Prathibha, Hongal, & Jyothi (Prathibha, Hongal, & Jyothi, 2017) have recommended utilizing advancing innovation. Checking natural variables is the focal point to improve the yield of productive harvests. The proposal (Skouby & Lynggaard, 2014) is a four-layer model that joins and interfaces the components by sending innovations.

Kumar *et al.* [20] have suggested a novel picture acknowledgment and route framework providing exact and brisk messages. These messages are as sound to outwardly tested individuals with the goal that they can explore effectively. The use of the proposed design comprises of two fundamental modules- Intelligent Navigation Module and Face Recognition Module. The proposed technique is split further with the assistance of ROC investigation.

The system [21] is a distributed computing engineering for an intelligent transportation framework that has four layers. The correspondence layer contains a transportation stratum for the sharing of data between the end-client. In the transportation stratum, there are two processors for preparing the information. First is the principle processor, the subsequent one is the backup processor. The fundamental processor will share the information with the customers in the scope of a specially appointed system or to a cloud-based server utilizing Internet administrations. The traditional cloud is dependable on the information authority stratum.

ANASTACIA [22] will build up a reliable by-structure autonomic security system that permits testing, approving, and enhancing security plans to the organization and upkeep. The system depends on assorted empowering agents to progressively coordinate. They send client security inclinations, encourage the organization of nearby operators, and implement security in diversified situations dependent on SDN/NFV and IoT systems.

Khanna & Anand [23] suggested an IoT-based cloud incorporated into an intelligent stopping framework. The proposed Smart Parking framework comprises of an on-location sending of an IoT module that screens and signalizes the condition of accessibility of each single parking spot. A versatile application permits an end client to check the accessibility of parking spots and book a stopping space as needs arise.

Fazio *et al.* [24] have analyzed Big Data issues. The problems have emerged from talks about various storage advancements, improving information stockpiling, questioning, and recovery. The capacity engineering couples both the Document and Object-oriented Storage Systems approaches in Big Data stockpiling. It misuses the Cloud processing innovation to profit the adaptability and unwavering quality. From the perspective of the Cloud client, information accumulated from the observing foundation is structured by the Sensor Web Enablement (SWE) determinations characterized by the Open Geospatial Consortium (OGC).

USE CASES

Doukas [25] suggested a stage-dependent on Cloud Computing for the executives of portable and wearable social insurance sensors. The system shows the IoT worldview applied to unavoidable medicinal services. The methodology assessment of a constant telemonitoring framework provides vision into the technology. The created structure comprises chiefly of two sections- the sensors that gather and transmit signals like temperature, movement, and heartbeat information and the cloud foundation for putting away and dealing with the data. Two arrangements created obtained readings. In the wearable system, the creators have utilized material accelerometers, a temperature sensor, and a heartbeat chest lash by Polar. The portable sensors are associated with a material variant of the Arduino open equipment microcontroller stage called LilyPad. The Cloud part comprises of a Java EE application that gives both the administration graphical interface and the interfaces for the correspondence with the sensors.

Li F., *et al.* [26] suggested utilizing Topology and Orchestration Specification for Cloud (TOSCA). It is another standard for cloud administration to determine the parts and designs of IoT applications. The creators exhibit the attainability of utilizing TOSCA. It indicates a run of the mill IoT application in building mechanization like the Air Handling Unit (AHU). The regular IoT segments examples include displaying entryways, and the channel required for communication for application arrangement will likewise be determined.

The system [27] is an exhaustive cloud-IoT medicinal services framework to engage discouraged patients over their treatment procedure. The creators have made a system comprising of all wellbeing entertainers for sharing and teaming up the information and administration on the single stage. The patient wears a checking gadget that gathers physical and rest-exercise data. These observing gadgets can be sensors/RFID labels set on the human body. Sensors/RFID labels can be worn as remain solitary gadgets or can be incorporated with adornments, applied as modest patches on the skin, covered up in the client's garments or shoes, or even embedded in the client's body hence making WBASN. Every hub in the WBASN is fit for detecting, testing, preparing, and remotely conveying at least one physiological sign. It can likewise assist with deciding the client's area, segregate among the client's states.

The framework [28] has two sections- the wearable and versatile sensors. These devices gather and transmit signals like circulatory strain, temperature, movement, and heartbeat information of a patient through cell phones to the Internet. The collected data are forwarded to the cloud framework for putting away and dealing with the data. The work [29] is a voice pathology identification framework. It is inside the observing structure utilizing nearby paired examples. It is also an extraordinary learning machine classifier to recognize the pathology. The databases employ Massachusetts Eye and Ear Infirmary (MEEI) database and the Saarbrucken Voice Database (SVD). A convenient voice recorder with Bluetooth innovation recorded the played examples at an inspecting recurrence of 11.25 kHz. The recordings were transferred to a cell phone at a later stage. There are 53 typical examples in the MEEI database and an excess of 1500 specimens in the SVD. The numbers for the neurotic sample are larger than 500 and 1500, separately.

Kaur & Maheshwari [30] recommends some techniques to change the present into a "Smart City." The systems include six fundamental key points - transport, correspondences, and different administration doings. The technique depends on three elemental standards - correlation, reconciliation, and collaboration. The framework will permit inhabitants and organizations with shared access to information and data about schools, streets, emergency clinics, structures, transport frameworks, vitality, and so forth.

The system [31] is a biometrics-based IoT framework. It needs to start to finish security systems ranging from various layers, including the gadget layer, omnipresent correspondence layer, a cloud layer, application, administrations, to partner layer.

The work [32] acquires the multi-occupant character of cloud to empower an idea of virtual verticals, rather than physically disconnected vertical arrangements. In virtual verticals, each IoT arrangement client possesses a disconnected structure. They can modify their physical surroundings and gadgets while sharing the hidden processing assets and middleware administrations with different clients. The methodology depends on extensible space middle people that handle area explicit gadgets and information models. Multi-inhabitant, adjustable provisioning of area explicitly control applications are used by the space middle people and the IoT PaaS engineering. The usage of IoT PaaS engineering depends on an open-source PaaS arrangement—WSO2. The WSO2 benefits legitimately utilized in our execution are ESB, Data Services, Governance Registry, and Identity server. JMS is the fundamental message-arranged middleware API, upheld by WSO2 Message Broker.

Cloud4IoT [33] provides two fundamental highlights. The first is the IoT Roaming use case. It underpins the programmed arrangement and re-setup of IoT Gateways. The successive component is the Application Scaling use case for a Data rationale and preparing an application sent on the edge layer. The Central Cloud runs on devoted servers and offers IaaS administration executed utilizing the Open Source OpenStack stage. The OpenStack condition, arranged for High Availability (HA), is made out of 3 Controller hubs, 2 Compute hubs. The register servers (HP ProLiant DL380 Gen9) are outfitted with 2xCPU Intel Xeon E5-2630 v3 2.4 GHz 8Cores/16Threads, 96GB RAM, 2x500 GB SATA 7.2K HDD. The controller servers (HP ProLiant DL360e Gen8) are furnished with 1xCPU Intel Xeon E5-2407 v2 2.4 GHz 4Cores/4Threads, 32GB RAM, 2x1TB SATA 7.2K HDD. The OpenStack Block Storage administration (ash) is incorporated into OpenStack by methods for HP LeftHand iSCSI SAN and offering 11TB of capacity limit.

Three surely understood stockpiling clouds are Amazon S3, Microsoft Windows Azure Blob Storage (Azure Blob), and Aliyun Open Storage Service (Aliyun OSS) [34]. Nature of Service assessment, Availability assessment, Responsiveness assessment, and security assessment is executed on the database.

The assessments of the physical memory catch are demonstrated in another study [5]. The memory dump can give potential to elective techniques for recuperating the login accreditations and log and metadata documents of legal content. The memory dump is a selective strategy to recover the running procedure and system data. The PIDs could help the examiner in acquiring information related to the customer application during further examination of the physical memory dumps. The nearness of the ancient rarities in the memory dump additionally implies the antiques located in the swap documents. Thus, the dormant memory pages are being swapped out of the memory to the hard disk during the framework's ordinary activity.

CHALLENGES

Security

Security is a risk provided that an interloper will make his way into the system in one way or another. Then, the impostor most likely deals with everything inside the framework. The dangers increment colossally when these frameworks are associated with the Internet.

The proposed framework [35] assesses six measurable parameters - the pinnacle signal-to-commotion proportion, mean square blunder, bit mistake rate, auxiliary likeness, essential substance, and connection.

Another work [36] measures its reception, expectation investigation of physical exercises, efficiency, and security. From the outcomes obtained, the general reaction between the neighborhood database server and Cloud server farm remains practically consistent with the ascent in the number of clients. For expectation examination, if the outcomes gathered continuously for the investigation of physical exercises surpass any of the parameter furthest reaches of the characterized edge esteem. This procedure leads to an alarm sent to the medicinal services faculty.

Sangpetch & Sangpetch [37] recommended a security setting system which applies versatile security settings to follow information of intrigue. The proposed arrangement can accomplish responsibility and track data spread, including gadgets, administrations, and gatherings that have the duty and potential lawful risk. It could help influence the permitted angles to empower wellbeing IoT selection.

Chifor *et al.* [38] recommended a lightweight approval stack for shrewd home IoT applications. A Cloud-associated gadget transfers input directions to a client's advanced mobile phone for approval. This engineering is client gadget driven and addresses security issues with regards to an untrusted Cloud stage. IoT Kaa is a multiple open-source IoT cloud platform adopted. The creators used the Java implementation open-sourced by eBay to implement the Fast ID Online (FIDO) protocol.

A study [39] utilizes Software-characterized Networking (SDN) for controlling traffic streams inside the system. It also offloads traffic examination errands to an intelligent Cloud-based Traffic Analyzer (CbTA). The analyzer utilizes a publicly supported information base for distinguishing system dangers and assaults. It is an adaptable, cost-effective, and effectively deployable answer for verifying distinctive system situations.

Availability

Aura [40] is an exceptionally restricted IoT based distributed computing model. Quality enables customers to utilize cloud-IoT and other figuring gadgets. The methodology gives limited calculation ability from undiscovered registering assets. Calculations done on Aura are exceptionally adaptable, giving customers full control to begin, stop, move, and restart computation close by gadgets as the customers move between various physical areas. To exhibit the possibility of Aura, the authors have ported a lightweight adaptation of MapReduce to run on IoT gadgets. Aura framework incorporates an Android application as the M-Agent, a work area based Java application as the controller, and a few virtual IoT gadgets running Contiki OS.

Zhang *et al.* [41], recommended a deliberation revolving around the information.

It focuses on replication, conservation, and uprightness of flood information. It empowers straightforward enhancement for the region and timely service deals in an appropriated stage, called the Global Data Plane (GDP). Its establishment is the idea of a solitary author affixing log, combined with an area free directing. It also overlays multicast and more significant level interfaces.

The system [42] is an adaptable IoT Cloud alliance vitality methodology for advancing the distribution of geologically restricted smart sensors. The IoT Cloud suppliers are interconnected to give all-inclusive decentralized detection conditions. In this, the aggregate is driven by requirements and understandings in a pervasive framework. The work considers a unique calculation method. The method is ready to improve vitality manageability in a unified IoT Cloud biological system.

He *et al.* [43] suggested a multilayered vehicular information cloud stage by utilizing distributed computing and IoT advancements. Two imaginative vehicular information cloud benefits include a smart leaving cloud administration and vehicular information mining cloud administration. Two altered information-digging models for the vehicular information mining cloud administration are Naïve Bayes and a Logistic Regression model.

Cloud4IoT [33] empowers the idea of Infrastructure as Code in the IoT setting. It enables IoT tasks with the adaptability and versatility of Cloud administrations. Besides, it moves customarily concentrated Cloud structures towards an increasingly circulated and decentralized calculation worldview. The various leveled engineering of Cloud4IoT has a focal Cloud stage and different remote edge Cloud modules supporting devoted gadgets. Cloud4IoT uses a few Open Source advancements for containerization and executions of benchmarks, conventions, and administrations for the IoT. CLOUDQUAL [34] is a model with quality measurements that govern administrations. CLOUDQUAL contains six quality measurements.

The proposal [44] is structured and actualized a productive plan called syncopy (synchronous duplicate) in HDFS(Hadoop Distributed File System) to direct continuous synchronization for documents with copies among various Hadoop bunches to accomplish high information accessibility and unwavering quality. The clients assured better opportunities to approach their information documents from one of the synchronized Hadoop groups.

The contribution [45] is a virtualization approach that bolsters a wide range of reliability examples and executes them as the requests of the application. The creators have actualized the virtualization system utilizing the Sixth Sense cloud stage with good assessment results on steadfastness measurements, for example, appreciable accessibility and the likelihood of disappointment on request.

The work [46] is cost-productive accessibility ensured for IoT administration chains over fog-center cloud systems. They suggested a productive accessibility Virtual Network Functions implanting system. The measure of accessibility improvement potential per unit cost (IPC), to quantify the accessibility improvement capability of a VNF is adopted. The measurement utilized discovers VNFs that have the most potential to improve the administration's unwavering quality inside a restricted asset required. In light of IPC, they structure a cost-effective VNF repetition assignment plot.

FUTURE DIRECTIONS

The incorporated IoT explicit difficulties include protection, participatory detection, information investigation, GIS-based representation, and Cloud registering. The registering separated from the standard WSN challenges includes design, vitality productivity, security, conventions, and Quality of Service. The ultimate objective is to have Plug n' Play brilliant articles conveyed in any condition with interoperable support enabling them to mix with others around them. Institutionalization of recurrence groups and conventions assumes an urgent job in achieving this objective.

The precision of analytic outcomes dependent on the ECG signal [11] should be improved to give an increasingly dependable ailment determination. The system [12] improves by providing an effective security system utilizing cryptographic calculations giving better security to the medicinal information on the cloud database. The proposal [13] improves by providing syntactic interoperability among heterogeneous IoT gadgets.

Another contribution [36] can address the issue of burden adjusting and data conveyance all through the Cloud servers, executing high-security calculations. Similarly, another work [31] can be intertwining multimodal non-obtrusive biometrics progressively to verify IoT ventures. This biometrics may incorporate face, discourse, and walk.

The viability of a vehicular cloud [43] relies on versatility to deal with a powerful change in the number of vehicles. The vehicular clouds must have the option to deal with traffic spikes or unexpected requests brought about by exceptional occasions or circumstances. Higher advancement in streamlining calculations that arrange virtual machines, extra room, and system data transfer capacity to adjust the server's outstanding tasks at hand and improve processing asset usage on the vehicular mists is required. As vehicles are frequently progressing, the vehicular systems administration correspondence is usually discontinuous or inconsistent. The new components expected to upgrade the unwavering quality with decreased traffic overhead is required. Further, the endeavors on institutionalization and security expected and assets for executing vehicular information is a necessity.

Two situations are considered for future work [44]. It is conceivable that the remote Hadoop bunch holding grind copies is down throughout refreshing the objective record. For a situation like this, syncopy will not have the option to synchronize the remote record copy since it sends the segment of restored information straightforwardly to the isolated Hadoop bunch. This dilemma is encountered when clients are annexing new information to target documents. Even though the clients are just permitted to affix the latest toward the finish of target documents in a Hadoop group, clients can erase target records if necessary.

The proposal [45] is a recuperation instrument for critical situations. The structure is a recuperation instrument that is simpler than the proposed methodology. Some of the virtual administration's activities have to be improved.

Bellavista & Zanni [3] suggested an adaptable design for the IoT. This scalable support system is vigorous w.r.t administration and asset provisioning. The revealed outcomes show that the proposed arrangement, because of MQTT and CoAP interworking, can ensure versatile help likewise for compelled gadgets. It does ensure by protecting the high message conveyance rate during engaged conditions. It can happen without producing activity peculiarities. The creators are further examining asset usage advancement as far as CPU and memory utilization and improved security support utilizing mix with Datagram Transport Layer Security (DTLS).

The framework [7] permits the profiting of both SQL-like and non-SQL DB arrangements. It ensures high security and productivity for the administration of data inside a Cloud. Simultaneously, a circulated non-SQL DB gives an overall augmentation to the framework. The creators might want to proceed with their work concerning request cooperation utilizing testbed using the CLEVER middleware with detecting augmentations and SEDNA as a non-SQL database for Big Data stockpiling.

REFERENCES

[1] B. Kantarci, and H.T. Mouftah, "Sensing services in cloud-centric Internet of Things: A survey, taxonomy and challenges", *IEEE International Conference on Communication Workshop (ICCW),* 2015, pp. 1865-1870 London, UK.
[http://dx.doi.org/10.1109/ICCW.2015.7247452]

[2] A. Taherkordi, and F. Eliassen, "Scalable modeling of cloud-based IoT services for smart cities", *IEEE International Conference on Pervasive Computing and Communication Workshops (PerCom Workshops),* 2016, pp. 1-6 Sydney, NSW, Australia.

[http://dx.doi.org/10.1109/PERCOMW.2016.7457098]

[3]   P. Bellavista, and A. Zanni, "Towards better scalability for IoT-cloud interactions via combined exploitation of MQTT and CoAP", In: *2nd International Forum on Research and Technologies for Society and Industry Leveraging a better tomorrow (RTSI)*, Bologna, Italy, 2016, pp. 1-6. [http://dx.doi.org/10.1109/RTSI.2016.7740614]

[4]   L. Jiang, "An IoT-Oriented Data Storage Framework in Cloud Computing Platform", *IEEE Trans. Industr. Inform.*, vol. 10, no. 2, pp. 1443-1451, 2014. [http://dx.doi.org/10.1109/TII.2014.2306384]

[5]   Y.Y. Teing, A. Dehghantanha, K.K.R. Choo, and L.T. Yang, "Forensic investigation of P2P cloud storage services and backbone for IoT networks: BitTorrent Sync as a case study", *Comput. Electr. Eng.*, vol. 58, pp. 350-363, 2017. [http://dx.doi.org/10.1016/j.compeleceng.2016.08.020]

[6]   J.D. Bokefode, A.S. Bhise, P.A. Satarkar, and D.G. Modani, "Developing a secure cloud storage system for storing IoT data by applying role based encryption", In: *12th International Multi-Conference on Information Processing-2016*, Bangalore, 2016, pp. 43-50. [http://dx.doi.org/10.1016/j.procs.2016.06.007]

[7]   M. Fazio, A. Celesti, M. Villari, and A. Puliafito, "The need of a hybrid storage approach for iot in paas cloud federation", *28th International Conference on Advanced Information Networking and Applications Workshops*, 2014, pp. 779-784 Victoria, BC, Canada. [http://dx.doi.org/10.1109/WAINA.2014.162]

[8]   J.S. Fu, Y. Liu, H.C. Chao, B.K. Bhargava, and Z.J. Zhang, "Secure data storage and searching for industrial IoT by integrating fog computing and cloud computing", *IEEE Trans. Industr. Inform.*, vol. 14, no. 10, pp. 4519-4528, 2018. [http://dx.doi.org/10.1109/TII.2018.2793350]

[9]   S.W. Kum, J. Moon, T. Lim, and J.I. Park, "A novel design of IoT cloud delegate framework to harmonize cloud-scale IoT services", *International Conference on Consumer Electronics (ICCE)*, 2015, pp. 247-248 Las Vegas, NV, USA.

[10]   N. Ambika, "Methodical IoT-Based Information System in Healthcare", In: *Smart Medical Data Sensing and IoT Systems Design in Healthcare*, chinmay chakraborthy, Ed., IGI Global: Bangalore, India, 2020, pp. 155-177.

[11]   Z. Yang, Q. Zhou, L. Lei, K. Zheng, and W. Xiang, "An IoT-cloud based wearable ECG monitoring system for smart healthcare", *J. Med. Syst.*, vol. 40, no. 12, p. 286, 2016. [http://dx.doi.org/10.1007/s10916-016-0644-9] [PMID: 27796840]

[12]   P.M. Kumar, S. Lokesh, R. Varatharajan, G.C. Babu, and P. Parthasarathy, "Cloud and IoT based disease prediction and diagnosis system for healthcare using Fuzzy neural classifier", *Future Gener. Comput. Syst.*, vol. 86, pp. 527-534, 2018. [http://dx.doi.org/10.1016/j.future.2018.04.036]

[13]   S. Jabbar, F. Ullah, S. Khalid, M. Khan, and K. Han, "Semantic interoperability in heterogeneous IoT infrastructure for healthcare", *Wirel. Commun. Mob. Comput.*, vol. 2017, pp. 1-10, 2017. [http://dx.doi.org/10.1155/2017/9731806]

[14]   S. Sharma, K. Chen, and A. Sheth, "Toward practical privacy-preserving analytics for IoT and cloud-based healthcare systems", *IEEE Internet Comput.*, vol. 22, no. 2, pp. 42-51, 2018. [http://dx.doi.org/10.1109/MIC.2018.112102519]

[15]   Y.E. Gelogo, H.J. Hwang, and H.K. Kim, "Internet of things (IoT) framework for u-healthcare system", *Int. J. Smart Home*, vol. 9, no. 11, pp. 323-330, 2015. [http://dx.doi.org/10.14257/ijsh.2015.9.11.31]

[16]   P. Verma, and S.K. Sood, "Cloud-centric IoT based disease diagnosis healthcare framework", *J. Parallel Distrib. Comput.*, vol. 116, pp. 27-38, 2018.

[http://dx.doi.org/10.1016/j.jpdc.2017.11.018]

[17]   M. Tao, J. Zuo, Z. Liu, A. Castiglione, and F. Palmieri, "Multi-layer cloud architectural model and ontology-based security service framework for IoT-based smart homes", *Future Gener. Comput. Syst.,* vol. 78, pp. 1040-1051, 2018.
[http://dx.doi.org/10.1016/j.future.2016.11.011]

[18]   G. Suciu, "Smart cities built on resilient cloud computing and secure internet of things", *19th International Conference on Control Systems and Computer Science,* 2013, pp. 513-518 Bucharest, Romania.
[http://dx.doi.org/10.1109/CSCS.2013.58]

[19]   J. Pacheco, and S. Hariri, "IoT security framework for smart cyber infrastructures", *in IEEE 1st International Workshops on Foundations and Applications of Self* Systems (FAS* W) , Augsburg, Germany,* pp. 242-247, 2016.
[http://dx.doi.org/10.1109/FAS-W.2016.58]

[20]   P.M. Kumar, "Intelligent face recognition and navigation system using neural learning for smart security in Internet of Things", *Cluster Comput.,* vol. 22, no. 4, pp. 1-12, 2017.

[21]   D. Singh, M. Singh, I. Singh, and H.J. Lee, "Secure and reliable cloud networks for smart transportation services", *17th International Conference on Advanced Communication Technology (ICACT),* 2015, pp. 358-362 Seoul, South Korea.
[http://dx.doi.org/10.1109/ICACT.2015.7224819]

[22]   S. Ziegler, A. Skarmeta, J. Bernal, E. E. Kim, and S. Bianchi, "ANASTACIA: Advanced networked agents for security and trust assessment in CPS IoT architectures", *in Global Internet of Things Summit (GIoTS), Geneva, Switzerland,* pp. 1-6, 2017.
[http://dx.doi.org/10.1109/GIOTS.2017.8016285]

[23]   A. Khanna, and R. Anand, "IoT based smart parking system", *International Conference on Internet of Things and Applications (IOTA),* 2016, pp. 266-270 Pune, India.
[http://dx.doi.org/10.1109/IOTA.2016.7562735]

[24]   M. Fazio, A. Celesti, A. Puliafito, and M. Villari, "Big data storage in the cloud for smart environment monitoring", *6th International Conference on Ambient Systems, Networks and Technologies (ANT-2015),* vol. 52, 2015, pp. 500-506 London, UK.
[http://dx.doi.org/10.1016/j.procs.2015.05.023]

[25]   "Bringing IoT and cloud computing towards pervasive healthcare", *in Sixth International Conference on Innovative Mobile and Internet Services in Ubiquitous Computing , Palermo, Italy,* pp. 922-926, 2012.

[26]   F. Li, M. Vögler, M. Claeßens, and S. Dustdar, "Towards automated IoT application deployment by a cloud-based approach", *6th International Conference on Service-Oriented Computing and Applications,* 2013, pp. 61-68 Koloa, HI, USA.
[http://dx.doi.org/10.1109/SOCA.2013.12]

[27]   S. Tyagi, A. Agarwal, and P. Maheshwari, *"A conceptual framework for IoT-based healthcare system using cloud computing," in 6th International Conference-Cloud System and Big Data Engineering.* Confluence: Noida, India, 2016, pp. 503-507.

[28]   M.M. Hassan, H.S. Albakr, and H. Al-Dossari, "A cloud-assisted internet of things framework for pervasive healthcare in smart city environment", *1st International Workshop on Emerging Multimedia Applications and Services for Smart Cities,* 2014, pp. 9-13 Orlando, Florida, USA.
[http://dx.doi.org/10.1145/2661704.2661707]

[29]   G. Muhammad, S.M.M. Rahman, A. Alelaiwi, and A. Alamri, "Smart health solution integrating IoT and cloud: A case study of voice pathology monitoring", *IEEE Commun. Mag.,* vol. 55, no. 1, pp. 69-73, 2017.
[http://dx.doi.org/10.1109/MCOM.2017.1600425CM]

[30]   M.J. Kaur, and P. Maheshwari, "Building smart cities applications using IoT and cloud-based architectures", *International Conference on Industrial Informatics and Computer Systems,* 2016, pp. 1-5 Sharjah, United Arab Emirates.
[http://dx.doi.org/10.1109/ICCSII.2016.7462433]

[31]   M.S. Hossain, "Toward end-to-end biometrics-based security for IoT infrastructure", *IEEE Wirel. Commun.,* vol. 23, no. 5, pp. 44-51, 2016.
[http://dx.doi.org/10.1109/MWC.2016.7721741]

[32]   F. Li, M. Vögler, M. Claeßens, and S. Dustdar, "Efficient and scalable IoT service delivery on cloud", *IEEE sixth international conference on cloud computing,* 2013, pp. 740-747 Santa Clara, CA, USA.

[33]   D. Pizzolli, "Cloud4iot: A heterogeneous, distributed and autonomic cloud platform for the iot", *IEEE International Conference on Cloud Computing Technology and Science (CloudCom),* 2016, pp. 476-479 Luxembourg City, Luxembourg.
[http://dx.doi.org/10.1109/CloudCom.2016.0082]

[34]   X. Zheng, P. Martin, K. Brohman, and L. Da Xu, "Cloudqual: A quality model for cloud services", *IEEE Trans. Industr. Inform.,* vol. 10, no. 2, pp. 1527-1536, 2014.
[http://dx.doi.org/10.1109/TII.2014.2306329]

[35]   M. Elhoseny, "Secure medical data transmission model for IoT-based healthcare systems", *IEEE Access,* vol. 6, pp. 20596-20608, 2018.
[http://dx.doi.org/10.1109/ACCESS.2018.2817615]

[36]   P.K. Gupta, B.T. Maharaj, and R. Malekian, "A novel and secure IoT based cloud centric architecture to perform predictive analysis of users activities in sustainable health centres", *Multimedia Tools Appl.,* vol. 76, no. 18, pp. 18489-18512, 2017.
[http://dx.doi.org/10.1007/s11042-016-4050-6]

[37]   O. Sangpetch, and A. Sangpetch, "Security Context Framework for Distributed Healthcare IoT Platform", *International Conference on IoT Technologies for HealthCare,* 2016, pp. 71-76 Västerås, Sweden.
[http://dx.doi.org/10.1007/978-3-319-51234-1_11]

[38]   B.C. Chifor, I. Bica, V.V. Patriciu, and F. Pop, "A security authorization scheme for smart home Internet of Things devices", *Future Gener. Comput. Syst.,* vol. 86, pp. 740-749, 2018.
[http://dx.doi.org/10.1016/j.future.2017.05.048]

[39]   I. Hafeez, "Cloud-based Security as a Service for Smart IoT Environments",

[40]   R. Hasan, M.M. Hossain, and R. Khan, "Aura: An iot based cloud infrastructure for localized mobile computation outsourcing", *3rd IEEE International Conference on Mobile Cloud Computing, Services, and Engineering,* 2015, pp. 183-188 San Francisco, CA, USA.
[http://dx.doi.org/10.1109/MobileCloud.2015.37]

[41]   "The cloud is not enough: Saving iot from the cloud", In: *7th Workshop on Hot Topics in Cloud Computing (HotCloud 15),* Santa curz, CA, 2015, pp. 1-7.

[42]   M. Giacobbe, A. Celesti, M. Fazio, M. Villari, and A. Puliafito, "A sustainable energy-aware resource management strategy for IoT Cloud federation", *IEEE International Symposium on Systems Engineering (ISSE),* 2015, pp. 170-175 Rome, Italy.
[http://dx.doi.org/10.1109/SysEng.2015.7302751]

[43]   W. He, G. Yan, and L. Da Xu, "Developing vehicular data cloud services in the IoT environment", *IEEE Trans. Industr. Inform.,* vol. 10, no. 2, pp. 1587-1595, 2014.
[http://dx.doi.org/10.1109/TII.2014.2299233]

[44]   T. Yeh, and H. Lee, "Enhancing availability and reliability of cloud data through syncopy", In: *IEEE International Conference on Internet of Things (iThings), and IEEE Green Computing and Communications (GreenCom) and IEEE Cyber, Physical and Social Computing (CPSCom),* Taipei, Taiwan, 2014, pp. 125-131.

[http://dx.doi.org/10.1109/iThings.2014.27]

[45] K.S. Dar, A. Taherkordi, and F. Eliassen, "Enhancing dependability of cloud-based IoT services through virtualization", *IEEE First International Conference on Internet-of-Things Design and Implementation (IoTDI)*, 2016, pp. 106-116 Berlin, Germany.
[http://dx.doi.org/10.1109/IoTDI.2015.38]

[46] Ngoc-Thanh Dinh and Younghan Kim, *An Efficient Availability Guaranteed Deployment Scheme for IoT Service Chains over Fog-Core Cloud Networks*, 2018.

SUBJECT INDEX

S

Z

www.ingramcontent.com/pod-product-compliance
Lightning Source LLC
Chambersburg PA
CBHW080020240326

41598CB00075B/601